TEACHER'S PET PUBLICATIONS

LITPLAN TEACHER PACK
for
The Color Purple
based on the book by
Alice Walker

Written by
Christina Stone

© 2008 Teacher's Pet Publications
All Rights Reserved

Copyright Teacher's Pet Publications 2008

Only the student materials in this unit plan (such as worksheets, study questions, and tests) may be reproduced multiple times for use in the purchaser's classroom.

For any additional copyright questions, contact Teacher's Pet Publications.

www.tpet.com

TABLE OF CONTENTS - *The Color Purple*

About The Author	4
Introduction	6
Unit Objectives	8
Reading Assignment Sheet	9
Unit Outline	10
Study Questions (Short Answer)	13
Quiz/Study Questions (Multiple Choice)	25
Pre-reading Vocabulary Worksheets	53
Lesson One (Introductory Lesson)	77
Non-fiction Assignment Sheet	91
Oral Reading Evaluation Form	89
Writing Assignment 1	95
Writing Assignment 2	101
Writing Assignment 3	109
Project	79
Writing Evaluation Form	96
Vocabulary Review Activities	121
Extra Writing Assignments/Discussion ?s	111
Unit Review Activities	122
Unit Tests	127
Unit Resource Materials	187
Vocabulary Resource Materials	207

ABOUT THE AUTHOR

Alice Walker

Alice Walker was born and raised in Eatonton, Georgia. She was the eighth child in a family of sharecroppers and always felt labeled by living in the South. After high school, Walker went to Spelman College on a full scholarship and later attended Sarah Lawrence College in New York.

While in college, Walker was inspired by one of her professors to take part in the Civil Rights Movement. She worked in the South helping to register voters, promote children's programs, and work for welfare rights. She has since become known as a feminist but prefers the term womanist instead.

In 1965, Walker married a Jewish Civil Rights lawyer, and they became the first legally married inter-racial couple in Mississippi. During their marriage they received numerous threats from the Ku Klux Klan but persevered and took joy in the birth of their daughter. The two eventually divorced, and their daughter became an author as well.

Alice Walker remains active in environmental, feminist/womanist causes and issues of economic justice while continuing to write.

Major Works
Novels and short story collections:
 The Third Life of Grance Copeland (1970), *Everyday Use* (1973), *In Love and Trouble: Stories of Black Women* (1973), *Roselily* (1973), *Meridian* (1976), *The Color Purple* (1982), *You Can't Keep a Good Woman Down: Stories* (1982), *Beauty: When the Other Dancer Is the Self (1983), Am I Blue?* (1986), *To Hell With Dying* (1988), *The Temple of My Familiar* (1989), *Finding the Green Stone* (1991), *Possessing the Secret of Joy* (1992), *The Complete Stories* (1994), *By The Light of My Father's Smile* (1998), *The Way Forward Is with a Broken Heart* (2000), *Now Is The Time to Open Your Heart* (2005)

Poetry collections:
 Once (1968), *Revolutionary Petunias and Other Poems* (1973), *Good Night, Willie Lee, I'll See You in the Morning* (1979), *Horses Make a Landscape Look More Beautiful* (1985), *Her Blue Body Everything We Know: Earthling Poems* (1991), *Absolute Trust in the Goodness of the Earth* (2003), *A Poem Traveled Down My Arm: Poems And Drawings* (2003), *Collected Poems* (2005), *Poem at Thirty-Nine*

Non-fiction:
 In Search of Our Mothers' Gardens: Womanist Prose (1983), *Living by the Word* (1988), *Warrior Marks* (1993), *The Same River Twice: Honoring the Difficult* (1996), *Anything We Love Can Be Saved: A Writer's Activism* (1997), *Go Girl!: The Black Woman's Book of Travel and Adventure* (1997), *Pema Chodron and Alice Walker in Conversation* (1999), *Sent By Earth: A Message from the Grandmother Spirit After the Bombing of the World Trade Center and Pentagon* (2001), *Women We Are the Ones We Have Been Waiting For* (2006), *Mississippi Winter IV*

Awards
Pulitzer Prize for Fiction - 1983 (First African American woman to win)
National Book Award
O. Henry Award - 1986
Humanist of the Year - 1997
The Lillian Smith Award from the National Endowment for the Arts

The Rosenthal Award from the National Institute of Arts & Letters
The Radcliffe Institute Fellowship, the Merrill Fellowship, and a Guggenheim Fellowship
The Front Page Award for Best Magazine Criticism from the Newswoman's Club of New York
Inducted into the California Hall of Fame located at The California Museum for History, Women, and the Arts - 2006

INTRODUCTION *The Color Purple*

This LitPlan has been designed to develop students' reading, writing, thinking, and language skills through exercises and activities related to *The Color Purple*. It includes twenty lessons, supported by extra resource materials.

The **introductory lesson** prompts students to think about letter writing, the format in which the novel is written.

The **reading assignments** are approximately thirty pages each; some are a little shorter while others are a little longer. Students have approximately 15 minutes of pre-reading work to do prior to each reading assignment. This pre-reading work involves reviewing the study questions for the assignment and doing some vocabulary work for selected vocabulary words they will encounter in their reading.

The **study guide questions** are fact-based questions; students can find the answers to these questions right in the text. These questions come in two formats: short answer or multiple choice. The best use of these materials is probably to use the short answer version of the questions as study guides for students (since answers will be more complete), and to use the multiple choice version for occasional quizzes.

The **vocabulary work** is intended to enrich students' vocabularies as well as to aid in the students' understanding of the book. Prior to each reading assignment, students will complete a two-part worksheet for selected vocabulary words in the upcoming reading assignment. Part I focuses on students' use of general knowledge and contextual clues by giving the sentence in which the word appears in the text. Students are then to write down what they think the words mean based on the words' usage. Part II nails down the definitions of the words by giving students dictionary definitions of the words and having students match the words to the correct definitions based on the words' contextual usage. Students should then have an understanding of the words when they meet them in the text.

After each reading assignment, students will go back and formulate answers for the study guide questions. Discussion of these questions serves as a **review** of the most important events and ideas presented in the reading assignments.

After students complete reading of the work, there is a **vocabulary review** lesson which pulls together all of the fragmented vocabulary lists for the reading assignments and gives students a review of all of the words they have studied.

Following the vocabulary review, a lesson is devoted to the **extra discussion questions/writing assignments**. These questions focus on interpretation, critical analysis and personal response, employing a variety of thinking skills and adding to the students' understanding of the novel.

There is a **relationship project** in this unit. This project requires students to analyze the relationships in the novel and explain how these relationships help characters to grow and change throughout the story.

There are three **writing assignments** in this unit, each with the purpose of informing, persuading, or expressing personal opinions. The first writing assignment asks students to mimic Celie and write a personal narrative about something difficult they've endured. The second writing assignment asks students to persuade a friend to speak up for him or herself and find a voice as Celie does in the text. In the third assignment students will take on the role of a character in the novel and write from that perspective to inform others about the hardships experienced by that character.

There is a non-fiction **reading assignment**. Students must read non-fiction articles, books, etc. to gather information about the themes discussed in the novel.

The **review lesson** pulls together all of the aspects of the unit. The teacher is given four or five choices of activities or games to use which all serve the same basic function of reviewing all of the information presented in the unit.

The **unit test** comes in two formats: multiple choice or short answer. As a convenience, two different tests for each format have been included. There is also an advanced short answer unit test for advanced students.

There are additional **support materials** included with this unit. The **Unit Resource Materials** section includes suggestions for an in-class library, crossword and word search puzzles related to the novel, and extra worksheets. There is a list of **bulletin board ideas** which gives the teacher suggestions for bulletin boards to go along with this unit. In addition, there is a list of **extra class activities** the teacher could choose from to enhance the unit or as a substitution for an exercise the teacher might feel is inappropriate for his/her class. **Answer keys** are located directly after the **reproducible student materials** throughout the unit. The **Vocabulary Resource Materials** section includes similar worksheets and games to reinforce the vocabulary words.

The **level** of this unit can be varied depending upon the criteria on which the individual assignments are graded, the teacher's expectations of his/her students in class discussions, and the formats chosen for the study guides, quizzes and test. If teachers have other ideas/activities they wish to use, they can usually easily be inserted prior to the review lesson.

The student materials may be reproduced for use in the teacher's classroom without infringement of copyrights. No other portion of this unit may be reproduced without the written consent of Teacher's Pet Publications, Inc.

UNIT OBJECTIVES *The Color Purple*

1. Through reading the novel *The Color Purple*, students will learn about the power words can have in helping someone find her voice and discover who she really is.

2. Students will learn about gender roles and sexism while reading about women who endure hardships and use their relationships to find their strength.

3. Students will demonstrate their understanding of the text on four levels: factual, interpretive, critical, and personal.

4. Students will make connections with the material in the text and apply the lessons learned to their lives.

5. Students will be given the opportunity to practice reading aloud and silently to improve their skills in each area.

6. Students will answer questions to demonstrate their knowledge and understanding of the main events and characters in *The Color Purple* as they relate to the author's theme development.

7. Students will enrich their vocabularies and improve their understanding of the novel through the vocabulary lessons prepared for use in conjunction with the novel.

8. Students will demonstrate the ability to write effectively to inform by developing and organizing facts to convey information. Students will demonstrate the ability to write effectively to persuade by selecting and organizing relevant information, establishing an argumentative purpose, and by designing an appropriate strategy for an identified audience. Students will demonstrate the ability to write effectively to express personal ideas by selecting a form and its appropriate elements.

9. Students will read aloud, report, and participate in large and small group discussions to improve their public speaking and personal interaction skills.

READING ASSIGNMENTS *The Color Purple*

Date Assigned	Assignment	Completion Date
	Assignment 1 Entries 1-21	
	Assignment 2 Entries 22-35	
	Assignment 3 Entries 36-48	
	Assignment 4 Entries 49-60	
	Assignment 5 Entries 61-68	
	Assignment 6 Entries 69-75	
	Assignment 7 Entries 76-81	
	Assignment 8 Entries 82-90	

UNIT OUTLINE *The Color Purple*

1 Introduction Project Assignment PVR1	2 Study Questions 1 Gender Roles PVR2	3 Study Questions 2 Oral Reading Evaluation PVR3	4 Nonfiction Reading	5 Study Questions 3 Community Discussion PVR4
6 Study Questions 4 Writing #1 PVR5	7 Study Questions 5 Venn Diagram PVR6	8 Study Questions 6 Climax Analysis	9 Writing #2 PVR7	10 Speaker
11 Background Information	12 Study Questions 8 Character Timeline	13 Gender and Community Discussion	14 Writing Assignment #3	15 Extra Discussion Questions
16 Extra Discussion Questions Cont.	17 Musical Analysis	18 Vocabulary Review	19 Unit Review	20 Unit Test

Key: P = Preview Study Questions   V = Vocabulary Work   R = Read

STUDY GUIDE QUESTIONS

STUDY GUIDE QUESTIONS *The Color Purple*

Assignment 1
<u>Entries 1-21</u>
1. To whom does Celie address her letters?
2. What does Celie's father mean when he says, "You gonna do what your mammy wouldn't"?
3. What does Celie mean when she says she's "big"?
4. How many times has Celie given birth? Who is the father?
5. What does Celie believe has happened to her babies?
6. Who is Mr. ___?
7. Celie's father refuses to let Nettie marry Mr. ___ but says he can marry Celie. How does Celie's father describe her to Mr. _____?
8. Why do both Nettie and Celie work so hard to become educated?
9. What does Celie discover about her daughter? How does she make this discovery?
10. When Mr. ___ tells Celie that Nettie must leave their house, what does Celie give to Nettie? What does Nettie promise Celie she will do?
11. Who is Shug Avery?
12. Who is Sofia, and for what reason does she get pregnant?
13. Harpo's father and Celie advise Harpo to beat his wife. What happens when he does this?
14. Why is Celie jealous of Sofia?

Assignment 2
<u>Entries 22-35</u>
1. How does Shug end up staying with Mr. _____ and Sofia?
2. When does Celie realize her husband's first name is Albert?
3. How many children do Shug and Albert have together? Where are their children?
4. What causes Mr. _____ and Celie to feel close to each other when Mr. _____'s father comes to visit?
5. Why does Celie cherish the quilt she and Sofia are making?
6. What strange habit does Harpo suddenly develop?
7. Why does Sofia leave Harpo? Where does she go?
8. What kind of a business does Harpo start, and where does he open it?
9. Shug sings a song for Celie. What is the song about?
10. Celie tells Shug that Mr. ___ will beat her when she is gone. When Shug asks why, what is Celie's response?
11. Shug asks Celie if it bothers her when Albert and Shug sleep together. Celie tells her she doesn't mind. What are Celie's true feelings toward Shug?

Assignment 3

<u>Entries 36-48</u>

1. What does Mr. ___ tell Sofia about his children?
2. Who is Squeak, and how did she lose two of her teeth?
3. Why is Sofia in jail?
4. What is Sofia's job in jail? What is her attitude and mental state?
5. Who takes care of Sofia's children while she is in jail?
6. What is the plan for getting Sofia out of jail?
7. Why is Squeak sent to talk to the warden? What happens while Squeak is with him?
8. For whom does Sofia work when she is released from jail?
9. When Sofia finally gets to see her family after five years, how long does she get to visit with them? Why?
10. What about Shug's Christmas visit surprises Albert and Celie?
11. What happens between Shug and Celie when Albert and Grady take the car for a long drive?
12. What does Shug want Mary Agnes to do?

Assignment 4

<u>Entries 49-60</u>

1. What does Shug discover that Albert has been keeping from Celie?
2. What does Celie want to do when she discovers Mr._____ has been keeping her letters from Nettie all these years?
3. Why didn't Albert marry Shug after she had his three children?
4. How do Celie and Shug get the rest of Nettie's letters without Albert's realizing they have them?
5. Why did Albert keep Nettie's letters from Celie?
6. According to her letter, with whom does Nettie live?
7. Where does Nettie go with the Reverend and his family? Why?
8. Nettie thanks her old school teacher for something. What?
9. What does Celie discover about the two children she had with her father?
10. Why is Nettie so certain that their missionary work will be successful?
11. What surprises Nettie about slavery?
12. Why does Shug suggest making pants for Celie?

Assignment 5

<u>Entries 61-68</u>

1. How do the Olinka people first react to Nettie and the other missionaries?
2. What special gift did the Olinka people give to the missionaries at the end of the welcoming ceremony?
3. Why are the Olinka people confused about the relationships among the missionary family?
4. Why does Corrine ask Nettie to stop wearing her clothes and to start addressing her and Samuel as if she were their sister?

5. Why do Tashi's parents come to see Nettie?
6. According to her letters, how long has Nettie been in Africa?
7. Why are the Olinka happy to see there is a road being built to their village? What later upsets them about the road?
8. After her husband dies, Tashi's mother is made an honorary man. What important decision does this empower her to make?
9. What happens to the Olinka people when the government sells the land they own to a rubber factory in England?
10. Who does Corrine believe are Adam and Olivia's birth parents?
11. Why had Samuel urged Nettie to come to Africa?
12. What does Nettie tell Celie about their Pa?

Assignment 6
Entries 69-75
1. How does Celie's old house look when Shug takes her to visit her Pa there?
2. Celie's Pa explains that he has been more successful with running a business and becoming a wealthy black man than her real father. What has he done differently to avoid the lynching her real father got after finding success?
3. How does Nettie finally convince Corrine that Celie is the mother of Adam and Olivia, and that the two of them had met once a long time ago?
4. What happens to Corrine?
5. Why doesn't Celie write to God anymore?
6. What does Shug teach Celie about God?
7. How does Mr. _____ react when he learns Shug is leaving and is planning to take Celie with her?
8. What does Celie do that surprises everyone at the dinner table?
9. Who is leaving with Shug to go to Tennessee?
10. Who offers to take care of Suzie Q (Squeak and Harpo's little girl) while Squeak goes north to sing?
11. What does Mr. _____ say to Celie as she is leaving for Tennessee?
12. What does Celie do to Albert as she is leaving for Tennessee?

Assignment 7
Entries 76-81
1. After moving to Memphis, what type of business does Celie start? What is the name of the business?
2. Celie comes to visit Sofia and Harpo when Sofia's mother dies. What are Sofia and Harpo arguing about when Celie arrives?
3. What is Celie's explanation when Harpo says Mary Agnes is different?
4. What does Celie learn about Mr. _____ and how he's been living since she moved away?
5. What happens to make Sofia have feelings for Harpo once again?
6. Sofia tells Celie Mr. ___ was in bad shape after Celie left him. What happened to turn Mr. ___'s life around?

7. What happens to Nettie and Samuel's relationship when they travel to England?
8. How are the Olinka people treated after the rubber factory is built?
9. What does Tashi do that upsets Adam?

Assignment 8
Entries 82-90
1. What does Celie inherit when her stepfather dies?
2. What crushing news does Shug give Celie when she goes back to Memphis?
3. Why does Henrietta eat yams, even though she hates the taste?
4. What is the only piece of mail Mr. ___ puts directly into Celie's hands?
5. Who is Miss Eleanor Jane, and what type of relationship does Sofia have with her?
6. What reasons does Tashi give for refusing to marry Adam?
7. What does Adam do to prove his love and devotion to Tashi?
8. What does Albert ask Celie? What is her response?
9. With whom is Celie reunited with at the end of the novel?

STUDY GUIDE QUESTIONS ANSWER KEY *The Color Purple*

Assignment 1
Entries 1-21

1. To whom does Celie address her letters?
   She addresses her letters to God.

2. What does Celie's father mean when he says, "You gonna do what your mammy wouldn't"?
   Her father says this before he rapes his daughter since his wife is too sick to have sex. Celie's father means he will have sex with Celie.

3. What does Celie mean when she says she's "big"?
   She means that her stomach has grown large due to pregnancy.

4. How many times has Celie given birth? Who is the father?
   Celie has given birth twice, and Celie's father is the father of both children.

5. What does Celie believe has happened to her babies?
   She believes her father killed the first baby and sold the second to a man and his wife in Monticello.

6. Who is Mr. ___?
   Mr. ___ is a man from church who is interested in marrying Nettie. His wife was killed, and he has three children in need of a mother.

7. Celie's father refuses to let Nettie marry Mr. ___ but says he can marry Celie. How does Celie's father describe her to Mr. _____?
   Celie's father says she is ugly, dumb, and unable to have any more children, but she is a hard worker and is good with children.

8. Why do both Nettie and Celie work so hard to become educated?
   Nettie and Celie understand they will have to be smart to get away from the life they are living.

9. What does Celie discover about her daughter? How does she make this discovery?
   Celie discovers that her daughter is still alive. While in town, Celie sees a little girl that looks just like Celie and her daddy. When Celie asks the child's name, the little girl's mother tells Celie that the child's name is Pauline, but she calls her Olivia. Olivia is the name Celie had embroidered on her daughter's diapers.

10. When Mr. ___ tells Celie that Nettie must leave their house, what does Celie give to Nettie? What does Nettie promise Celie she will do?
    Celie gives her sister the name of the Reverend who has her daughter, in the hope that the Reverend's wife will help Nettie. Nettie promises to write letters to Celie.

11. Who is Shug Avery?
    She is a singer who performs in the area. Mr. ___'s sisters allude to a romantic relationship between Mr. ___ and Shug.

12. Who is Sofia, and for what reason does she get pregnant?
    Sofia is the girl Harpo loves. She gets pregnant because that is the only way her father will allow her to marry Harpo.

13. Harpo's father and Celie advise Harpo to beat his wife. What happens when he does this?
    Sofia fights back. Harpo's face is covered in bruises, he has a cut lip, and his eye is swollen shut.

14. Why is Celie jealous of Sofia?
    Celie tells Sofia that she is jealous of her strength and will to fight back.

Assignment 2
<u>Entries 22-35</u>

1. How does Shug end up staying with Mr. _____ and Sofia?
   Mr. _____ brings Shug home because she is sick and needs someone to care for her.

2. When does Celie realize her husband's first name is Albert?
   Celie has never called her husband by his first name and is only vaguely aware that Albert is his name until Shug calls him that.

3. How many children do Shug and Albert have together? Where are their children?
   They have three children who are living with Shug's mother.

4. What causes Mr. _____ and Celie to feel close to each other when Mr. _____'s father comes to visit?
   When Mr. _____'s father says mean things about Shug, both Celie and her husband get very defensive. Celie enjoys having Shug around, and so does Mr. _____. Their shared love and adoration for Shug helps them to feel close to each other for the first time.

5. Why does Celie cherish the quilt she and Sofia are making?
   Shug donated her yellow dress for pieces of the quilt. Celie wants the quilt so she has a piece of Shug near her always.

6. What strange habit does Harpo suddenly develop?
   He eats all the time, stuffing himself as often as possible.

7. Why does Sofia leave Harpo? Where does she go?
   She leaves Harpo because he is always trying to control her. She takes their children and goes to live with her sisters.

8. What kind of a business does Harpo start, and where does he open it?
   Harpo opens a jukejoint in his and Sofia's home.

9. Shug sings a song for Celie. What is the song about?
   The song is about a woman who has a no-good man doing her wrong again.

10. Celie tells Shug that Mr. ___ will beat her when she is gone. When Shug asks why, what is Celie's response?
    Celie says it is because she is Celie, not Shug.

11. Shug asks Celie if it bothers her when Albert and Shug sleep together. Celie tells her she doesn't mind. What are Celie's true feelings toward Shug?
    Celie loves Shug and has developed an attraction to her. Celie is also jealous of Albert's relationship with Shug.

Assignment 3
<u>Entries 36-48</u>

1. What does Mr. ___ tell Sofia about his children?
   Mr. ___ tells Sofia that his two girls are pregnant and gone, and his son Bud is in and out of jail.

2. Who is Squeak, and how did she lose two of her teeth?
   Squeak is Harpo's girlfriend. She called Sofia a bitch and told her to stop dancing with her man. She then slapped Sofia, and Sofia punched her back, knocking out two of her teeth.

3. Why is Sofia in jail?
   Sofia was in town with her kids when the mayor's wife, a white woman, saw how clean and well-kept Sofia's kids were. When she asked Sofia if she would like to be her maid, Sofia said, "Hell no." The mayor was offended and slapped Sofia. Sofia punched the mayor. Police then came, beat Sofia severely, and threw her in jail.

4. What is Sofia's job in jail? What is her attitude and mental state?
   Sofia works in the prison laundry and is a model prisoner. She says she acts just like Celie and does anything they ask her to without complaint. However, she is starting to go crazy from acting in this way and thinks about murder all the time.

5. Who takes care of Sofia's children while she is in jail?
   Harpo's girlfriend (Squeak) and Sofia's sisters take care of her six children.

6. What is the plan for getting Sofia out of jail?
   The plan is to tell the warden that Sofia is happy in jail since she does less work there than at home. Squeak plans to tell the warden that the way to really punish her is to make her work for a white woman. This way Sofia can have a better life, and the warden can feel like he is making her suffer.

7. Why is Squeak sent to talk to the warden? What happens while Squeak is with him?
   Squeak is sent to talk with the warden because he is her uncle. Her mother had three illegitimate children by a white man, the brother of the warden. While she is there the warden rapes her after recognizing who she is.

8. For whom does Sofia work when she is released from jail?
   Ironically, Sofia goes to work for the mayor's wife, the woman she had rudely refused three years before, causing the incident that had landed her in jail.

9. When Sofia finally gets to see her family after five years, how long does she get to visit with them? Why?
   Sofia only gets to visit with her family for about fifteen minutes because Miss Millie insists that she needs Sofia to ride with her.

10. What about Shug's Christmas visit surprises Albert and Celie?
    She surprises Albert and Celie with her new husband, Grady.

11. What happens between Shug and Celie when Albert and Grady take the car for a long drive?
    Shug and Celie are intimate and fall asleep in the same bed.

12. What does Shug want Mary Agnes to do?
    Shug wants Mary Agnes (Squeak) to sing in public, and Shug is planning on having Mary Agnes sing at Harpo's with her on stage.

Assignment 4
<u>Entries 49-60</u>

1. What does Shug discover that Albert has been keeping from Celie?
   Shug notices that when she walks to the mailbox with Albert he often takes a letter with funny stamps and puts it straight in his jacket pocket. She gets suspicious and discovers Albert has been keeping Nettie's letters from Celie.

2. What does Celie want to do when she discovers Mr._____ has been keeping her letters from Nettie all these years?
   She wants to kill him.

3. Why didn't Albert marry Shug after she had his three children?
   His father and brother told him Shug was trash because she had three kids. There was no way of proving they were all actually Albert's.

4. How do Celie and Shug get the rest of Nettie's letters without Albert's realizing they have them?
   Shug gets the keys to Albert's trunk where all the letters are hidden. They steam open the envelopes and take out the letters, putting the empty envelopes back in the trunk.

5. Why did Albert keep Nettie's letters from Celie?
   On the day Nettie left, Albert followed her and tried to kiss her and drag her into the woods. She fought him and hurt him enough for him to leave her alone. He told Nettie that because of that Celie would never hear from Nettie and Nettie would never hear from Celie.

6. According to her letter, with whom does Nettie live?
   She lives with Reverend Samuel, his wife Corrine, and their two children (Olivia and Adam).

7. Where does Nettie go with the Reverend and his family? Why?
   She goes to Africa with the Reverend and his family, to care for Olivia and Adam (since the woman who was supposed to care for the children got married and could not go).

8. Nettie thanks her old school teacher for something. What?
   Nettie is thankful her teacher taught her to learn on her own and helped foster in her a desire for learning.

9. What does Celie discover about the two children she had with her father?
   They are both growing up in a house full of love. Samuel and Corrine adopted them but have no idea that Nettie, the person helping to care for their children, is their aunt and sister.

10. Why is Nettie so certain that their missionary work will be successful?
    She is certain it will be successful because they are black people going into Africa working towards the common goal of uplifting black people everywhere.

11. What surprises Nettie about slavery?
    That Africans used to capture their own people and sell them into the slave trade surprises Nettie.

12. Why does Shug suggest making pants for Celie?
    Celie is mad about Mr. ___'s keeping Nettie's letters from her--and wants to kill him. To distract Celie from her anger and grief, Shug suggests making Celie some pants.

Assignment 5
Entries 61-68

1. How do the Olinka people first react to Nettie and the other missionaries?
   The Olinka people are curious about their clothes and ask questions about the relationship of the children to Nettie and Corrine. They also ask if Nettie and Corrine are both Samuel's wives. They seem pretty welcoming and have built huts for them to live in.

2. What special gift did the Olinka people give to the missionaries at the end of the welcoming ceremony?
   They were given a roof made of roofleaf for their hut.

3. Why are the Olinka people confused about the relationships among the missionary family?
   They are confused because Adam and Olivia look like Nettie but belong to Samuel and Corrine.

4. Why does Corrine ask Nettie to stop wearing her clothes and to start addressing her and Samuel as if she were their sister?
    Corrine wants it made clear to the Olinka people that she alone is Samuel's wife and the mother of the children.

5. Why do Tashi's parents come to see Nettie?
    The Olinka people do not believe girls should be educated. Tashi's parents know she has been spending a lot of time with Olivia and that she is becoming quiet and thoughtful. They come to talk to Nettie because they feel Tashi's association with Olivia is changing Tashi in ways that will keep her from fitting in with her community and their values.

6. According to her letters, how long has Nettie been in Africa?
    Nettie has been in Africa for over five years.

7. Why are the Olinka happy to see there is a road being built to their village? What later upsets them about the road?
    At first the Olinka are happy to see there is a road being built to their village since it will make travel much quicker and easier to and from the village. However, they are later upset to learn that the road is not stopping at their village but going straight through it and destroying several buildings, including the school and church. The road builders have guns and use force to ensure they road is built despite the fact the Olinka people own the land.

8. After her husband dies, Tashi's mother is made an honorary man. What important decision does this empower her to make?
    Tashi's mother decides that Tashi should be educated and try to learn as much as possible.

9. What happens to the Olinka people when the government sells the land they own to a rubber factory in England?
    The Olinka people are forced to pay rent on the land and pay a tax on the water they get from the land.

10. Who does Corrine believe are Adam and Olivia's birth parents?
    Corrine believes Nettie and Samuel are Adam and Olivia's birth parents. She does not know they are actually Celie's children by Celie's own father.

11. Why had Samuel urged Nettie to come to Africa?
    Samuel had urged Nettie to come to Africa because he thought Adam and Olivia were Nettie's children, and he wanted her to be with them.

12. What does Nettie tell Celie about their Pa?
    Nettie tells Celie that the man they have always thought of as their Pa is not really their father. Their mother was married to another man who owned a store and land. After he was killed by white people, she remarried while her two daughters were still babies. The second man she married is the man they always thought of as their Pa.

Assignment 6
Entries 69-75
1. How does Celie's old house look when Shug takes her to visit her Pa there?
    The house looks like a white person's house. It's large and beautiful with blooming flowers landscaping the yard.

2. Celie's Pa explains that he has been more successful with running a business and becoming a wealthy black man than her real father. What has he done differently to avoid the lynching her real father got after finding success?
   Celie's Pa offers the white people money. He gives them a third of his profit and pays a white boy to run his store. That way, the white people get money from a black man's success and see a white boy, not a black man, running a successful store.

3. How does Nettie finally convince Corrine that Celie is the mother of Adam and Olivia, and that the two of them had met once a long time ago?
   Nettie finds a quilt that Corrine made using old pieces of the children's clothing. One of those patches was made from the fabric Corrine was buying the day she met Celie and had a conversation with her. Seeing the fabric finally makes Corrine remember the day she met Celie, the real mother of her two children.

4. What happens to Corrine?
   Corrine's health continues to decline, and she dies.

5. Why doesn't Celie write to God anymore?
   Celie doesn't write to God anymore because she thinks God is a man. All the men in her life have always been no-good and let her down, just as she feels God has.

6. What does Shug teach Celie about God?
   Shug tells Celie that God isn't a man or a woman, but an It. She tells Celie to get the image of God being an old white man out of her head and to start seeing God in the world that is all around her. She tells her God is inside everyone, and they just have to find it. She says that God loves all people and just wants to be loved and appreciated back.

7. How does Mr. _____ react when he learns Shug is leaving and is planning to take Celie with her?
   He forbids it and says it will be over his dead body.

8. What does Celie do that surprises everyone at the dinner table?
   She speaks out against her husband, saying how horrible he was to her and how awful his children were. She also stabs him in the hand with her knife as he tries to slap her.

9. Who is leaving with Shug to go to Tennessee?
   Mary Agnes (Squeak) is going to Tennessee with Shug and Celie.

10. Who offers to take care of Suzie Q (Squeak and Harpo's little girl) while Squeak goes north to sing?
    Sofia offers to take care of Suzie Q.

11. What does Mr. _____ say to Celie as she is leaving for Tennessee?
    He insults her in every way possible. He insults her appearance, her personality, her ability to cook, and the way she keeps a house.

12. What does Celie do to Albert as she is leaving for Tennessee?
    She curses Albert, telling him everything he touches will crumble until he does right by her.

Assignment 7
Entries 76-81

1. After moving to Memphis, what type of business does Celie start? What is the name of the business?
   Celie begins her own pants business. She calls it "Folkspants, Unlimited."

2. Celie comes to visit Sofia and Harpo when Sofia's mother dies. What are Sofia and Harpo arguing about when Celie arrives?
   Sofia wants to be a pallbearer in her mother's funeral (along with her other sisters), but Harpo thinks it is a man's job and is worried about what people will think.
3. What is Celie's explanation when Harpo says Mary Agnes is different?
   Celie tells Harpo and Sofia that Mary Agnes smokes a lot of the reefer that Grady grows in the back yard.
4. What does Celie learn about Mr. _____ and how he's been living since she moved away?
   Celie learns Mr. _____ has been working very hard in the fields and keeping the house up nicely.
5. What happens to make Sofia have feelings for Harpo once again?
   Sofia sees how kindly Harpo treats his father while he is dealing with Celie's absence and begins to have feelings for him once again.
6. Sofia tells Celie Mr. ___ was in bad shape after Celie left him. What happened to turn Mr. ___'s life around?
   Harpo made Mr. ___ send Celie the rest of Nettie's letters. Right after that, Mr. ___ started to feel better.
7. What happens to Nettie and Samuel's relationship when they travel to England?
   They realize their love for each other and get married.
8. How are the Olinka people treated after the rubber factory is built?
   They are forced to move to a barren area of land that is without water six months of the year. In this time, they must pay the factory for water. There is also no more roofleaf left, leaving the Olinka people without their item of worship.
9. What does Tashi do that upsets Adam?
   She has gone through with the tribal ceremony of cutting or scarring her face. She has also had the female initiation ceremony

Assignment 8
Entries 82-90

1. What does Celie inherit when her stepfather dies?
   Celie inherits the house, land, and dry goods store when her stepfather dies. Nettie and Celie actually have owned all of this since their mother died, but she doesn't find out about it until her stepfather's will is read years later.
2. What crushing news does Shug give Celie when she goes back to Memphis?
   Shug tells Celie she is in love with a 19 year old boy, Germaine, who joined her band recently.
3. Why does Henrietta eat yams, even though she hates the taste?
   Henrietta is very sick, and there is no definite cure. The only thing her family knows to do is feed her a lot of yams to improve her health and prevent her from dying. Her sickness is consistent with Malaria, though it is never confirmed that this is what she is suffering from.
4. What is the only piece of mail Mr. ___ puts directly into Celie's hands?
   Mr. ___ gives her a telegram from the Department of Defense notifying Celie that a German mine has sunk the ship on which Nettie's family was traveling, off the coast of Gibraltar. No survivors have been discovered.

5. Who is Miss Eleanor Jane, and what type of relationship does Sofia have with her?
   Miss Eleanor Jane is the white girl Sofia practically raised while working for the mayor and his wife. She visits Sofia at her home on a regular basis. Eleanor Jane feels a connection with Sofia. She tries to be part of Sofia's life, while allowing Sofia to be part of hers as well. However, Sofia doesn't return the same feelings of love for Eleanor Jane, and though she likes her and appreciates her kindness, Sofia pushes Eleanor Jane away. Later, Eleanor Jane asks her mother why Sofia came to work for their family and realizes the injustice that has been done. Eleanor Jane then works for Sofia, cooking for Henrietta and taking care of her when she's sick.

6. What reasons does Tashi give for refusing to marry Adam?
   She is worried Americans will look down on her because of the scarification marks on her face and because of her very dark skin. She is also worried Adam will find someone else to love in America, and she will then be all alone in a strange country with no family.

7. What does Adam do to prove his love and devotion to Tashi?
   Adam has his face scarred to look like Tashi's.

8. What does Albert ask Celie? What is her response?
   Albert asks Celie to marry him again, but this time in spirit and flesh. She refuses and asks if they can just be friends.

9. With whom is Celie reunited with at the end of the novel?
   Much to Celie's surprise and delight, Nettie returns, and she is reunited with Nettie, Adam, and Olivia.

MULTIPLE CHOICE STUDY/QUIZ QUESTIONS
The Color Purple

Assignment 1
Entries 1-21

1. To whom does Celie address her letters?
    A. Nettie
    B. Her dead mother
    C. Herself
    D. God

2. What does Celie's father mean when he says, "You gonna do what your mammy wouldn't"?
    A. Celie's father means Celie will take care of her sister.
    B. Celie's father means that Celie will go to school.
    C. Celie's father means it is now Celie who will do the cooking and cleaning.
    D. Celie's father means he will have sex with Celie.

3. What does Celie mean when she says she's "big"?
    A. Celie means she is taller than her friends.
    B. Celie means she is pregnant.
    C. Celie means she is growing older.
    D. Celie means she is overweight.

4. How many times has Celie given birth? Who is the father?
    A. She has four children by the white man for whom her father works.
    B. She has three children by three different fathers.
    C. She has two children by her father.
    D. She has one child by the school teacher.

5. What does Celie believe has happend to her babies?
    A. Celie believes her father killed both babies.
    B. Celie believes her father sold both babies.
    C. Celie believes her father killed the first baby and sold the second.
    D. Celie believes God took both babies.

6. Who is Mr. ____ ?
    A. Mr. ____ is the preacher at Nettie's church.
    B. Mr. ____ is a man from church who is interested in marrying Nettie.
    C. Mr. ____ is the man who bought Celie's babies.
    D. Mr. ____ is the man who visits Celie on Sundays.

7. Celie's father refuses to let Nettie marry Mr. ____ but says he can marry Celie. How does Celie's father describe her to Mr. _____?
    A. He says she is ugly, dumb, and unable to have any more children. He also says she is a hard worker and good with children.
    B. He says she has able hips to help her bear children and do heavy labor. He also says she can sing and make a blueberry pie better than any he's tasted.
    C. He says she is quiet and will never talk back. He also says she doesn't need much to eat and can get by with only two dresses.
    D. He says she is well educated and a good Christian. He also says she keeps a clean house, can care for farm animals, and doesn't need many material items.

8. Why do both Nettie and Celie work so hard to become educated?
    A. Both girls are very competitive for the attention of their father and work hard to make him proud.
    B. Both girls are the first in their family to be allowed to attend school and are honored to have this opportunity.
    C. Both girls aspire to open their own school house when they are older.
    D. Both girls understand they will have to be smart to get away from the life they are living.

9. What does Celie discover about her daughter?
    A. Celie discovers her daughter is still alive.
    B. Celie discovers her daughter is being raised by a man and his wife who run the general store in Monticello.
    C. Celie discovers her daughter is in a orphanage in Georgia.
    D. Celie discovers her daughter is buried in the local cemetery.

10. When Mr. _____ tells Celie that Nettie must leave their house, what does Celie give to Nettie? What does Nettie promise Celie she will do?
    A. Celie gives her sister the name of the Reverend who has Celie's daughter, and Nettie promises to write letters to Celie.
    B. She gives her sister an old Bible to help her find her way, and in return Nettie promises to never abandon her faith.
    C. Celie gives her sister a quilt she made from scraps of their old dresses and in return Nettie promises to send money to Celie to help her run away from Mr. _____.
    D. She gives her sister a photograph of the two of them, and in return Nettie promises to visit at least twice a year.

11. Who is Shug Avery?
    A. She is a singer who travels the area performing. Mr. _____'s sisters allude to a romantic relationship between Mr. _____ and Shug.
    B. She is a school teacher who secretly continues to tutor Celie even though she is already married. She knows Celie is smart and helps her to keep learning to one day get away from Mr. _____.
    C. She is Mr. _____'s sister who comes to stay with them for a while. Her husband beat her and she ran away to the safety of her older brother.
    D. She is the wife of the Reverend. She helps Celie adjust to her new life as the wife of a selfish man and the mother of four children who hate her.

12. Who is Sofia?
    A. The woman who is taking care of the son Celie's father took away from her after he was born
    B. The girl Harpo gets pregnant and later marries
    C. The wife of the man who got Celie pregnant a third time
    D. Mr. _____'s youngest daughter who has decided to love Celie as though she were her mother

13. Harpo's father and Celie advise Harpo to beat his wife. What happens when he does this?
    A. Sofia falls and has to be taken to the hospital.
    B. Sofia leaves Harpo and their children to live with her sister.
    C. Sofia fights back.
    D. Sofia calls the police and has Harpo arrested.

14. Why is Celie jealous of Sofia?
    A. Celie tells Sofia that she is jealous of her ability to fight back.
    B. Celie is jealous of Sofia's natural beauty.
    C. Celie is jealous because Sofia was able to keep all her children.
    D. Celie tells Sofia that she is jealous of her relationsip with Harpo.

Assignment 2
Entries 22-35

1. How does Shug end up staying with Mr. _____ and Sofia?
   A. Shug's father dies and is buried near town. Mr. _____ tells her to stay with them while she is recovering from her grief.
   B. Mr. _____ and Harpo aren't making much money off their crops, so they ask Shug to come stay with them and let them manage her career in local clubs.
   C. Shug's car breaks down as she is passing through town. Since she is black, the town mechanic tells her it will take a few weeks for him to fix it. Mr. _____ invites her to stay with them while she waits.
   D. Mr. _____ goes to get her in his wagon one day after church when he hears she is sick.

2. When does Celie realize her husband's first name is Albert?
   A. Celie never knew her husband's name was Albert until Nettie told her.
   B. When Shug's father died, Celie heard the preacher call her husband "Albert."
   C. Celie has never called her husband by his first name and is only vaguely aware that Albert is his name until Shug calls him that.
   D. Celie only learns her husband's first name after he dies.

3. How many children do Shug and Albert have together? Where are their children?
   A. They have three children who live with Shug's mother.
   B. They have two children who live with Shug's youngest sister.
   C. They have five children, but three died. They live with Albert's sister.
   D. They have four children who live with two different adoptive families.

4. What causes Mr. _____ and Celie to feel close to each other when Mr. _____'s father comes to visit?
   A. Mr. _____'s father compliments Celie on her fine job of raising the kids and keeping a clean, well-run house, making the two feel proud.
   B. Mr. _____'s father talks about how much he loved and misses his dead wife, making Celie and her husband feel closer.
   C. Mr. _____'s father says rude things about the way Celie looks and the how stupid she is, and Mr. _____ stands up to defend her.
   D. Mr. _____'s father says mean things about Shug; both Celie and her husband get very defensive.

5. Why does Celie cherish the quilt she and Sofia are making?
   A. Though she thought she was unable to get pregnant, Celie realizes she is pregnant, and this quilt is for her new child.
   B. Shug donated her yellow dress for pieces. Celie wants the quilt so she has a piece of Shug near her always.
   C. This is the first quilt Celie has ever made. She is proud of the intricate design she and Sofia are making.
   D. Celie knows Sofia will be leaving soon, and this is the one thing she will have to remember her by.

6. What strange habit does Harpo suddenly develop?
   A. He sleeps on the floor instead of in bed with Sofia.
   B. He does the dishes and takes care of the children without being asked.
   C. He shaves his head completely bald.
   D. He eats all the time, stuffing himself as often as possible.

7. Why does Sofia leave Harpo? Where does Sofia go?
   A. Sofia leaves Harpo because he is always trying to control her. She takes their children and goes to live with her sisters.
   B. Sofia leaves Harpo because he is always trying to beat her. She takes their children and goes to live with her mother.
   C. Sofia leaves Harpo because he is always running around with other women. She takes their children and goes to live with her sisters.
   D. Sofia leaves Harpo because he is not working or helping her around the house. She takes their children and goes to live with her sisters.

8. What kind of a business does Harpo start, and where does he open it?
   A. Harpo opens a jukejoint in his and Sofia's home.
   B. Harpo opens a restaurant in his and Sofia's home.
   C. Harpo opens a meat-packing operation in his and Sofia's home.
   D. Harpo opens a brothel in his and Sofia's home.

9. Shug sings a song for Celie. What is the song about?
   A. The song is about a woman who murders her husband and gets away with it.
   B. The song is about a woman who is hurt a lot but is rewarded in the end.
   C. The song is about a woman who runs away and finds a better life.
   D. The song is about a woman who has a no-good man doing her wrong again.

10. Celie tells Shug that Mr. ___ will beat her when she is gone. When Shug asks why, what is Celie's response?
    A. Celie says it is because Mr. ___ is nicer when Shug is around.
    B. Celie says it is because she is Celie, not Shug.
    C. Celie says it is because Mr. ___ hates her.
    D. Celie says it is because she is Celie, not Nettie.

11. Shug asks Celie if it bothers her when Albert and Shug sleep together. Celie tells her she dosen't mind. What are Celie's true feelings toward Shug?
    A. Celies loves Shug but resents Shug for sleeping with Albert each night.
    B. Celie loves Shug and has developed an attraction to her. Celie is also jealous of Albert's releationship with Shug.
    C. Celie has no feelings for Shug but Celie is happy that Shug keeps Albert occupied.
    D. Celie hates Shug and is jealous of all the attention Shug gets from the men at the jukejoint.

Assignment 3
Entries 36-48

1. What does Mr. ___ tell Sofia about his children?
    A. Mr. ___ tells Sofia the oldest girl is in jail, the youngest girl is working as a missionary, and Bud is working at a dry-goods store.
    B. Mr. ___ tells Sofia the two girls are pregnant and gone, and his son, Bud, is in and out of jail.
    C. Mr. ___ tells Sofia the two girls married, and his son, Bud, is in the Army.
    D. Mr. ___ tells Sofia the oldest girl is pregnant with her third child, the youngest girl is teaching school, and Bud is in college.

2. Who is Squeak, and how did she lose two of her teeth?
    A. Squeak is Harpo's girlfriend. She was walking home from church when a white man pulled up in a car. He tried to take advantage of her, but she fought back, losing two teeth in the process.
    B. Squeak is Harpo's girlfriend. She called Sofia a bitch and told her to stop dancing with her man. She then slapped Sofia, and Sofia punched her back, knocking out two of her teeth.
    C. Squeak is Harpo's girlfriend. She was singing at the jukejoint one night when Sofia hit her with a bottle, knocking out two of her teeth.
    D. Squeak is Harpo's girlfriend. She talked back to Mr. _____ one night and he hit her, knocking out two of her teeth.

3. Why is Sofia in jail?
    A. Sofia attacks Squeak when she sees her hugging Harpo. Harpo pulls Sofia off his girlfriend, and Sofia's date slugs Harpo for touching Sofia. The place gets so rowdy, the police arrive and Sofia is arrested with a number of others.
    B. The store owner tries to cheat Sofia when she is buying cloth. She argues with him. He throws her out, keeping her money and not giving her any cloth. She bangs on the locked door and yells and is arrested for disrupting the peace.
    C. The mayor's wife asked Sofia if she would like to be her maid and Sofia said, "Hell no." The mayor was offended and slapped Sofia. She punched the mayor and was thrown in jail.
    D. Sofia is in town and begins to feel sick. She cannot find a Colored bathroom, so she sneaks into the white bathroom. On her way out, she gets caught by a shop owner who immediately calls the police.

4. What is Sofia's job in jail? What is her attitude and mental state?
   A. Sofia works in the prison laundry and fights with the other prisoners to protect herself. However, she is starting to go crazy from all the stress and beatings.
   B. Sofia works in the prison kitchen and is a model prisoner. However, she is starting to go crazy and thinks about murder all the time.
   C. Sofia works in the prison kitchen and has an occasional run-in with the warden. She is happy to be in prison because it is less work than being at home.
   D. Sofia works in the prison laundry and is a model prisoner. However, she is starting to go crazy and thinks about murder all the time.

5. Who takes care of Sofia's children while she is in jail?
   A. Squeak and Sofia's sisters take care of Sofia's children.
   B. Miz Millie and Sofia's sisters take care of Sofia's children.
   C. Squeak and Celie take care of Sofia's children.
   D. Squeak and Harpo take care of Sofia's children.

6. What is the plan for getting Sofia out of jail?
   A. To tell the warden Sofia is happy in jail and the way to really punish her is to make her work for a white woman
   B. To ask for parole for good behavior, pleading for Sofia to be back with her six children and under house arrest
   C. To get dynamite from the people building a nearby bridge and bust her out one night
   D. To try to make the case that Sofia is mentally unstable, getting her to a mental hospital or back home in the care of her family

7. Why is Squeak sent to talk to the warden? What happens while Squeak is with him?
   A. Squeak's father had done many favors for the warden, and Squeak thought this would give her the upper hand. The warden gets angry and beats Squeak for coming to him about Sofia.
   B. Squeak is sent because she related to the warden. While she is there, the warden rapes her.
   C. Squeak had dated the warden a few years back. While she is there, she sleeps with him again.
   D. Squeak is sent because her mother is the warden's maid. While she is there, she agrees that her mother will go without pay for six months if he releases Sofia.

8. For whom does Sofia work when she is released from jail?
   A. She works for the owner of the dry-goods store where he makes her do humiliating work.
   B. She works at the jukejoint making BBQ for customers.
   C. She works at the church doing God's work and repenting for her sins.
   D. She works for the same white woman who got her put in jail.

9. When Sofia finally gets to see her family after five years, how long does she get to visit with them? Why?
   A. Sofia gets to spend a week with her children because Miz Millie and her family are going out of town for the Christmas holiday.
   B. Sofia only gets to visit with her family for about fifteen minutes because Miz Millie insists that she needs Sofia to ride with her.
   C. Sofia gets to spend an afternoon with her children because Miz Millie is feeling guilty about keeping Sofia from her children.
   D. Sofia gets to spent the night with her children because Miz Millie is going out of town for the night.

10. What about Shug's Christmas visit surprises Albert and Celie?
    A. Shug has come to live with Albert and Celie, not just for a Christmas visit.
    B. Shug brings Albert's children as a surprise for Albert and Celie.
    C. Shug surprises Albert and Celie with a new car.
    D. Shug surprises Albert and Celie with her new husband, Grady.

11. What happens between Shug and Celie when Albert and Grady take the car for a long drive?
    A. Shug and Celie fight because Celie is jealous of Grady.
    B. Nothing happens between Shug and Celie even though they have strong feelings for each other.
    C. Shug kisses Celie and Celie tells Shug to never do that again.
    D. Shug and Celie are intimate and fall asleep in the same bed.

12. What does Shug want Mary Agnes to do?
    A. Shug wants Mary Agnes to go to college.
    B. Shug wants Mary Agnes to sing in public.
    C. Shug wants Mary Agnes to leave Harpo.
    D. Shug wants Mary Agnes to have a baby to make Harpo happy.

Assignment 4
Entries 49-60

1. What does Shug discover that Albert has been keeping from Celie?
   A. Shug discovers Albert has been keeping the truth about Celie's children from her.
   B. Shug discovers Albert has been keeping Celie's children from her.
   C. Shug discovers Albert has been keeping Nettie's letters from Celie.
   D. Shug discovers Albert has been keeping money from Celie's share of the jukejoint food sales.

2. What does Celie want to do when she discovers Mr._____ has been keeping her letters from Nettie all these years?
   A. She wants to kill him.
   B. She wants to humiliate him in front of Shug.
   C. She wants to leave him.
   D. She wants to confront him.

3. Why didn't Albert marry Shug after she had his three children?
   A. Shug told Albert she couldn't marry someone without any money, and the land he had to live on wasn't going to be enough to support her in the lifestyle she wanted.
   B. Shug made it clear she wanted no part in marrying Albert unless he wanted to follow her around the country to support her singing career.
   C. His father and brother told him Shug was trash since she had three kids and there was no way of proving they were all Albert's.
   D. His father wanted him to marry a good Christian and had already made arrangements with Mary Agnes's family for him to marry her.

4. How do Celie and Shug get the rest of Nettie's letters without Albert's realizing they have them?
   A. Shug confronts Albert about the letter and refuses to speak to him ever again if he doesn't come clean with Celie and let her have her letters.
   B. Shug leaves the key for Celie while she takes Albert to the jukejoint for the night to get drunk, thinking Celie should have enough time to read most of the letters.
   C. Celie and Albert go to church while Shug goes through Albert's trunk to find the letters, later hiding them under Celie's pillow for her to read that night.
   D. Shug gets the keys to Albert's trunk. They steam open the envelopes, taking out the letters and putting the empty envelopes back in the trunk.

5. Why did Albert keep Nettie's letters from Celie?
   A. On the day Nettie left, Albert tried to kiss her and drag her into the woods. When she was able to fight him off, he told her that she and Celie would never hear from each other again.
   B. Albert kept the letters from Celie because he knew she would sit and read them when she should be working.
   C. Albert wanted complete control over Celie, so he would not let her have contact with anyone in her family.
   D. Albert kept the letters from Celie because he didn't want Nettie to return to his house.

6. According to her letter, with whom does Nettie live?
   A. Nettie lives with the Reverend Samuel, his wife Corrine, and their two children (Olivia and Adam).
   B. Nettie lives with her Aunt Mary, Uncle John, and their seven children.
   C. Nettie lives with the school teacher and her husband.
   D. Nettie lives with Odessa, Sofia's sister.

7. Where does Nettie go with the Reverend and his family? Why?
   A. Nettie goes to India to care for Olivia and Adam.
   B. Nettie goes to China to care for Olivia and Adam.
   C. Nettie goes to England to care for Olivia and Adam.
   D. Nettie goes to Africa to care for Olivia and Adam.

8. Nettie thanks her old school teacher for something. What?
   A. Nettie is thankful her teacher taught her how to be patient with others when helping them learn new information.
   B. Nettie is thankful her teacher taught her how to read and write.
   C. Nettie is thankful her teacher taught her how to understand money and how to manage what she has to survive.
   D. Nettie is thankful her teacher taught her how to learn on her own and helped foster in her a desire for learning.

9. What does Celie discover about the two children she had with her father?
   A. Celie discovers her children are living in an orphanage outside of town.
   B. Celie discovers her children are dead.
   C. Celie discovers her children are living with their father's aunt.
   D. Celie discovers her children are alive and have been adopted by Samuel and Corrine.

10. Why is Nettie so certain that their missionary work will be successful?
    A. Nettie is certain they will succeed in their missionary work because they are black people going to Africa, working together to uplift black people everywhere.
    B. Nettie is certain they will succeed in their missionary work because God will lead them.
    C. Nettie is certain they will succeed in their missionary work because they have love in their hearts.
    D. Nettie is certain they will succeed in their missionary work because they are all very intelligent.

11. What surprises Nettie about slavery?
    A. That Africans used to capture their own people and sell them into the slave trade.
    B. America wasn't the only country that had slaves.
    C. Slaves used to be severely beaten and many died from cruel treatment.
    D. People used to be auctioned off like cattle at town markets.

12. Why does Shug suggest making pants for Celie?
    A. Shug wants pants for herself but she wants to see them on Celie first.
    B. Shug wants to distract Celie from her anger and grief.
    C. Shug thinks Celie will look nicer in pants.
    D. Shug wants Celie to make pants to earn her own money.

13. Why are the Olinka people confused about the relationships among the missionary famliy?
    A. They are confused because Samuel spends more time with Nettie than with Corrine and the children.
    B. They are confused because Adam and Olivia look like Nettie but belong to Samuel and Corrine.
    C. They are confused because Adam, Corrine, and Nettie all sleep in the same hut.
    D. They are confused because Olivia looks like Nettie and Adam looks like Corrine.

Assignment 5
Entries 61-68

1. How do the Olinka people first react to Nettie and the other missionaries?
    A. They are uneffected by the missionaries and go on with life as if they don't exist. They have seen many missionaries in their lifetimes and aren't impressed, nor bothered, by the arrival of Nettie and the others.
    B. They are curious about the missionaries and ask questions about the relationship of the children to Nettie and Corrine. They also ask if Nettie and Corrine are both Samuel's wives. They seem pretty welcoming and have built huts for them to live in.
    C. They are overjoyed the missionaries have finally arrived. They corresponded with Samuel in letters and were very happy to finally meet Corrine and the children since he spoke so highly of them. They have also prepared a feast in celebration of the occasion.
    D. They are angry that the missionaries have come to change their culture. They give Nettie and Corrine dirty looks, and the children are harassed by the other kids in the village. Very few people will talk to the missionaries, and they feel unwelcome.

2. What special gift did the Olinka people given to the missionaries at the end of the welcoming ceremony?
    A. They are given a hut twice the size of the Olinka chief.
    B. They were given a large knife for hunting.
    C. They were given a colorful quilt.
    D. They were given a roof made of roofleaf for their hut.

3. Why does Corrine ask Nettie to stop wearing her clothes and to start addressing her and Samuel as if she were their sister?
    A. Corrine wants it made clear to the Olinka people that she alone is Samuel's wife and the mother of the children.
    B. Corrine is worried the children are thinking of Nettie as their mother, and she doesn't want Samuel thinking of Nettie as anything but a sister.
    C. Corrine is worried because Samuel is looking at Nettie in an inappropriate way. Corrine wants Nettie in her old clothes and to let Samuel know he is like a brother to her.
    D. Corrine wants the Olinka people to view Nettie as her own person, not one of the children.

4. Why do Tashi's parents come to see Nettie?
   A. Tashi's parents come to invite Nettie to dinner to thank her for all she is doing to educate Tashi.
   B. Tashi's parents come to see Nettie because they are worried their daughter is changing because of her friendship with Olivia, and that Tashi's will not fit in with her community.
   C. Tashi's parents come to warn Nettie the chief is angry because she is teaching the girls in the village and that she must stop for her own safety.
   D. Tashi's parents come to see Nettie because they want Olivia and Nettie to teach Tashi's even though it is against Olinka belief to educate women.

5. According to her letters, how long has Nettie been in Africa?
   A. Nettie has been in Africa for almost 3 months.
   B. Nettie has been in Africa for over 5 years.
   C. Nettie has been in Africa a little less than 1 year.
   D. Nettie has been in Africa for nearly 10 years.

6. Why are the Olinka happy to see there is a road being built to their village? What later upsets them about the road?
   A. They are happy since it will finally allow for their village to have modern amenities like those found in larger cities. They are later upset to learn that the road is not sturdy enough to survive the rainy season and will be destroyed after only a few months of use.
   B. They are happy since it will make travel much quicker and easier to and from the village. They are later upset to learn the road is not stopping at their village but going straight through it and destroying several buildings.
   C. They are happy since it is providing work for many people of their village in a time when money is tight. They are later upset because the men do not pay them as promised, and the Olinka realize they worked hard for nothing in return.
   D. They are happy since it will allow for increased trade with neighboring villages, making survival in the rainy season much easier. They are later upset to learn they will have to pay a large fee to use the road, making trade nearly impossible.

7. After her husband dies, Tashi's mother is made an honorary man. What important decision does this empower her to make?
   A. She decides that Tashi should be educated and try to learn as much as possible.
   B. She decides that Tashi will not be given any further education, and Olivia must join the Olinka if she is to be friends with Tashi.
   C. She decides that Tashi will not take part in the female initiation ceremony.
   D. She will decide who Tashi will marry.

8. What happens to the Olinka people when the government sells the land they own to a rubber factory in England?
    A. They are forced to pay rent on the land and pay a tax on the water they get from the land.
    B. They must agree to work at the rubber factory, even though the conditions are horrible and they will receive no pay.
    C. They must find a new place to live or be killed.
    D. They are given a small purchase fee for the land which aids the people in finding a new place to rebuild.

9. Who does Corrine believe are Adam and Olivia's parents?
    A. Corrine believes Nettie and Mr. _____ are Adam and Olivia's birth parents.
    B. Corrine believes Celie and Albert are Adam and Olivia's birth parents.
    C. Corrine believes Nettie and Samuel are Adam and Olivia's birth parents.
    D. Corrine believes Celie and Samuel are Adam and Olivia's birth parents.

10. Why had Samuel urged Nettie to come to Africa?
    A. Samuel urged Nettie to come to Africa because he had fallen in love with her.
    B. Samuel urged Nettie to come to Africa because he thought Adam and Olivia were Nettie's children, and he wanted them to be together.
    C. Samuel urged Nettie to come to Africa because he saw how close she and Olivia were and thought it would make the journey easier for Olivia.
    D. Samuel urged Nettie to come to Africa because he knew Corrine would never be able to take care of the children.

11. What does Nettie tell Celie about their Pa?
    A. Nettie tells Celie he tried to rape her the day she left.
    B. Nettie tells Celie he is wanted for murder, and if he is arrested, they will be able to be together again.
    C. Nettie tells Celie their Pa is rich but he hid the money until all the children had left home.
    D. Nettie tells Celie the man they always thought of as their Pa is really not their father.

Assignment 6
Entries 69-75

1. How does Celi's old house look when Shug takes her to visit her Pa there?
    A. The house looks horrible. The yard hasn't been taken care of, and the house is obviously falling apart.
    B. The house looks well taken care of. It's been painted a few times and a garage has been added, but it still resembles the house Nettie grew up in.
    C. The house looks like a white person's house. It's large and beautiful with blooming flowers landscaping the yard.
    D. The house looks exactly like she remembered. The old car is still sitting out front, and the tire swing she and Nettie used to play on is still hung over the tree.

2. Celie's Pa explains that he has been more successful with running a business and becoming a wealthy black man than her real father. What has he done differently to avoid the lynching her real father got after finding success?
    A. He makes sure to follow all of the state laws and regulations.
    B. He pays all his taxes and makes sure to give money back to the community and to those in need.
    C. He works with the white people and asks their permission before he proceeds with any new business ideas.
    D. He offers the white people part of his profit so they aren't upset at his success.

3. How does Nettie finally convince Corrine that Celie is the mother of Adam and Olivia, and that the two of them had met once a long time ago?
    A. She tells her the same story every day about how Corrine met Celie in the dry-goods store. Each day Corrine says she can't remember, until she is on her death bed and in and out of consciousness. It is this time she finally remembers meeting Celie.
    B. She finds an old family photo tucked in the pages of her Bible. She shows Corrine the photo and helps her see the resemblance of Adam and Olivia in Celie. This photo helps Corrine to remember the face of the girl she met long ago in the store.
    C. She sprays a bit of old perfume on Corrine one day before church services. The smell reminds Corrine of a time long ago, and she is able to think back to the day she bought it, the very same day she met Celie at the store.
    D. She finds a quilt Corrine made using old pieces of the children's clothing. One of those patches was made from the fabric Corrine was buying the day she met Celie, which makes her remember the day she met her.

4. What happens to Corrine?
    A. Corrine leaves Samual and returns to England to live.
    B. Corrine kills herself becuase she believes Samual has been unfaithful to her.
    C. Corrine is placed in a sanatorium in Africa.
    D. Corrine's health continues to decline, and she dies.

5. Why doesn't Celie write to God anymore?
   A. Celie doesn't write to God anymore because she feels she is strong enough to handle her problems herself.
   B. Celie doesn't write to God anymore because she is writing to Shug.
   C. Celie doesn't write to God anymore because she can now write to Nettie.
   D. Celie doesn't write to God anymore because she thinks God is a man and all the men in her life are no-good and always let her down.

6. What does Shug teach Celie about God?
   A. Shug tells Celie that God isn't a man or a woman, but an It. She tells Celie God is inside everyone, and they just have to find it.
   B. Shug says God created sin and therefore doesn't mind if people stray from the right path everyone once in a while. She also says that God wants people to enjoy life and all He has created.
   C. She says God is for people who are dead or dying and the living should focus on living and experiencing the world. She also says religion is something created by white men, making it hard for her to believe.
   D. Shug tells Celie that God doesn't care about women and only listens to men. She also says that praying to Him each day and trying to live life for Him is ridiculous.

7. How does Mr. _____ react when he learns Shug is leaving and is planning to take Celie with her?
   A. He kicks Shug out of the house and tells her she is never allowed back again.
   B. He forbids it and says it will be over his dead body.
   C. He says he's glad to finally get rid of her and helps Shug pack Celie's bags.
   D. He begs Celie not to go, saying he needs her to take care of the house.

8. What does Celie do that surprises everyone at the dinner table?
   A. She smiles all through dinner and tells jokes, making everyone laugh. She also sings and dances after dinner, and is in the happiest mood anyone has ever seen.
   B. She refuses to say a prayer before the meal and leaves the room while everyone else blesses the meal. She also decides not to help clean up the meal once everyone is finished.
   C. She speaks out against her husband, saying how horrible he was to her and how awful his children were. She also stabs him in the hand with her knife as he tries to slap her.
   D. She cries in front of everyone, showing real emotion for the first time. She also tells everyone how much they mean to her and how she's appreciated their support while she was married to Albert.

9. Who else is leaving with Shug to go to Tennessee?
   A. Sofia
   B. Albert
   C. Mary Agnes
   D. Harpo

10. Who offers to take care of Suzie Q (Squeak and Harpo's little girl) while Squeak goes north to sing?
    A. Celie
    B. Odessa
    C. Sofia
    D. Albert

11. What does Mr. _____ say to Celie as she is leaving for Tennessee?
    A. Mr. ___ says he will kill her is she steps one foot off the porch.
    B. Mr. ___ tells her how much he will miss her.
    C. Mr. ___ says he is a fool, and if Celie will stay, he will change his ways.
    D. Mr. ___ insults her in every way possible.

12. What does Celie do to Albert as she is leaving?
    A. She puts a curse on him.
    B. She hits him.
    C. She smiles at him.
    D. She hugs him.

Assignment 7
Entries 76-81

1. After moving to Memphis, what type of business does Celie start? What is the name of the business?
    A. Celie begins her own pants business and she calls it "Folkspants, Unlimited."
    B. Celie begins her own laundry business and she calls it "Cleanclothes, Unlimited."
    C. Celie begins her own pants business and she calls it "Pantsfolks, Unlimited."
    D. Celie begins her own laundry business and she calls it "Cleanfolks, Unlimited."

2. Celie comes to visit Sofia and Harpo when Sophia's mother dies. Why are Harpo and Sofia arguing when Celie arrives?
    A. Sofia wants to be a pallbearer in her mother's funeral, but Harpo thinks it is a man's job.
    B. Harpo wants Sofia to cut off all connections with the white family, but Sofia still feels affection for the little girl and tries to help her when she can.
    C. Harpo wants to have another child, but Sofia thinks they've had enough children and refuses to have any more.
    D. Sofia wants Harpo to stand up to his father and refuse to work for him unless he pays him more, but Harpo is scared to talk to his father.

3. What is Celie's explanation when Harpo says Mary Agnes is different?
    A. Celie tells Harpo it is just his imagination.
    B. Celie tells Harpo it is because Mary Agnes is drinking all the time.
    C. Celie tells Harpo it is because Mary Agnes smokes a lot of the reefer that Grady grows in the back yard.
    D. Celie tells Harpo it is because Mary Agnes is on her own now, and she can take care of herself.

4. What does Celie learn about Mr. _____ and how he's been living since she moved away?
    A. Mr. _____ hired a young woman to live with him to help around the house and keep up with the cooking.
    B. Mr. _____ hired help for the fields and got a job in town working for the county jail. He makes enough money to live from his job and is creating a savings account with the money made off his land.
    C. Mr. _____'s older sister moved in with her three children after her husband was killed. Mr. _____ has been supporting the family for a few months now.
    D. Mr. _____ has been working very hard in the fields and keeping the house up nicely.

5. What happens between Harpo and Sofia to make them have feelings for each other once again?
    A. Harpo's daughter with Mary Agnes dies at the age of nine. Sofia is so moved by his feelings for this young child that she can't help but develop feelings for him again.
    B. Sofia becomes pregnant with their sixth child, and their relationship grows as Harpo works hard to care for Sofia during this difficult pregnancy.
    C. Sofia sees how kindly Harpo treats his father when he is dealing with Celie's absence and begins to have feelings for him once again.
    D. Harpo sold his jukejoint to have enough money to buy Sofia out of the remaining portion of her jail sentence. She is so impressed with his compassion that she falls in love with him again.

6. Sofia tells Celie Mr. ___ was in bad shape after Celie left him. What happened to turn Mr. ___'s life around?
    A. Sending Celie the rest of her letters from Nettie
    B. Writing to Nettie to explain why Celie hasn't written in all these years
    C. Finding God and attending church services regularly
    D. Seeing Celie again and apologizing

7. What happens to Nettie and Samuel's relationship when they travel to England?
    A. They argue about whether or not to send the children to school in England or take them back to Africa and damage their friendship.
    B. They realize their love for each other and get married.
    C. They realize it is too hard to be friends without Corrine around and decide to go their separate ways.
    D. They grow closer in their friendship and decide to always stay in touch no matter what happens.

8. How are the Olinka people treated after the rubber factory is built?
   A. They are rewarded by the factory owners for giving up their land with gifts from the white world, like radios, bikes, jeans, mirrors, and toys. They are also paid for their time working in the factory and are permitted to live in the baracks provided.
   B. They are forced to move to a barren area of land that is without water six months of the year. In this time, they must pay the factory for water. There is also no more roofleaf left, leaving the Olinka people without their item of worship.
   C. They are given the opportunity to either work for the factory or continue to live on their land. They are permitted to use the resources of the factory and can make a nice living by trading with the factory owners. They are also allowed to retain their tribal traditions.
   D. They are required to work for the factory, even though the conditions are poor and several people have been injured as a result of the dangerous work. They also are prohibited from practicing their tribal traditions and must adopt the ways of the white people.

9. What does Tashi do that upsets Adam?
   A. She has decided to attend college in England in the fall. He is worried she will not adjust to the new lifestyle after living in a small tribal region in Africa for her whole life.
   B. She is working for the rubber factory running heavy tree-cutting machinery and putting her life in danger for the profit of others, completey giving up on her education.
   C. She has run away from the tribe to live with the *mbeles* and rebel against the rubber factory. Her life may be in danger if the factory uses force to stop the tribal people from protesting.
   D. She has gone through with the tribal ceremony of cutting or scarring her face and she has had the female initiation ceremony.

Assignment 8
Entries 82-90

1. What does Celie inherit when her stepfather dies?
    A. The farm land, a horse, and $10,000
    B. Over $5000 worth of debt and a stepsister
    C. The house, land, and dry-goods store
    D. Nothing

2. What crushing news does Shug give Celie when she goes back to Memphis?
    A. Shug tells Celie she is in love with a 19 year old boy.
    B. She is slowly dying from cancer
    C. Shug tells Celie she is going out on the road for a 3 year tour.
    D. Shug tells Celie she is going back to Albert to get married.

3. Why does Henrietta eat yams, even though she hates the taste?
    A. She is on a strict diet in order to lose enough weight to become a lounge singer like Shug and Mary Agnes.
    B. She is very superstitious and believes yams will help her maintain her light skinned color, helping her to look younger and more attractive.
    C. She read in the Bible yams were grown in the Garden of Eden and feels closer to God when she eats this vegetable.
    D. She is very sick and the only thing her family knows to do is feed her a lot of yams to improve her health and prevent her from dying.

4. What is the only piece of mail Mr. ___ puts directly into Celie's hands?
    A. He gives Celie a letter from Olivia.
    B. He gives her a telegram from the African government notifying Celie that Nettie was killed in Africa.
    C. He gives Celie a letter he found in the bottom of his trunk.
    D. He gives her a telegram from the Department of Defense notifying Celie that a German mine has sunk the ship on which Nettie's family was traveling.

5. Who is Miss Eleanor Jane, and what type of relationship does Sofia have with her?
    A. Eleanor Jane is the daughter of the mayor and his wife. Sofia hates Eleanor Jane because she represents a life of enslavement to a white family. Sofia is always rude to her.
    B. Eleanor Jane is the daughter of the mayor and his wife. Sofia loves Eleanor Jane since she raised her as her own child. Their relationship becomes strained as Eleanor Jane gets older and realizes it is not acceptable for her to have such a close relationship with a black woman.
    C. Eleanor Jane is Sofia's oldest daughter. She resents Sofia for abandoning her as a child and finds it hard to even talk to her. Sofia is persistent in trying to make amends with Eleanor Jane in order to make things right in her life.
    D. Eleanor Jane is the daughter of the mayor and his wife. Eleanor feels a connection with Sofia, but Sofia pushes her away. After Eleanor Jane finds out why Sofia came to work for their family, she realizes the injustice that has been done. Eleanor Jane then goes to work for Sofia.

6. What reasons does Tashi give for refusing to marry Adam?
    A. She is already engaged to an Olinka tribal leader and feels obligated to honor her commitment. She is also fearful Adam will want children; she knows she is unable to reproduce after the female initiation ceremony.
    B. She is angry that Adam went to England and knows he will one day leave her again if it suits his own needs. She is also angry he waited so long to find her and feels this may be a sign he doesn't love her.
    C. She is worried Americans will look down on her because of the scarification marks on her face and her very dark skin. She is also worried Adam will find someone else to love in America, and she will then be left all alone.
    D. She is scared to leave the Olinka village and leave behind the customs and traditions she values. She is also scared Americans will think she is dumb since she is from Africa.

7. What does Adam do to prove his love and devotion to Tashi?
    A. Adam goes through the Olinka male initiation ceremony.
    B. Adam stays with Tashi in Africa.
    C. Adam performs the Olinka marriage dance before the entire Olinka tribe.
    D. Adam has his faced scarred to look like Tashi's.

8. What does Albert ask Celie? What is her response?
    A. He asks her to marry him again, but this time in spirit and flesh. She says no and asks if they can just be friends.
    B. He asks her if she hates him for all the times he mistreated her over the years. She says she has finally forgiven him.
    C. He asks her if he can make shirts to go with her pants to sell them as sets. She says he can make shirts, but she won't sell them as part of her business.
    D. He asks her to help him win back Shug. She says she loves Shug too and is trying to win her back herself.

9. Who is Celie reunited with at the end of the novel?
    A. Shug and her two children
    B. Her mother
    C. Her old school teacher
    D. Nettie, Olivia, and Adam

ANSWER KEY: STUDY QUESTIONS *The Color Purple*

	1	2	3	4	5	6	7	8
1	D	D	B	C	B	C	A	C
2	D	C	B	A	D	D	A	A
3	B	A	C	C	A	D	C	D
4	C	D	D	D	B	D	D	D
5	C	B	A	A	B	D	C	D
6	B	D	A	A	B	A	A	C
7	A	A	B	D	A	B	B	D
8	D	A	D	D	A	C	B	A
9	A	D	B	D	C	C	D	D
10	A	B	D	A	B	C		
11	A	B	D	A	D	D		
12	B		B	B		A		
13	C			B				
14	A							

VOCABULARY WORKSHEETS

VOCABULARY ASSIGNMENT 1 *The Color Purple*

Part I: Using Prior Knowledge and Contextual Clues

Below are the sentences in which the vocabulary words appear in the text. Read the sentence. Use any clues you can find in the sentence combined with your prior knowledge, and write what you think the underlined words mean on the lines provided.

1. I tell Nettie to keep at her books. It be more then a <u>notion</u> taking care of children ain't even yourn.

   _____

2. My little girl she look up and sort of frown. She <u>fretting</u> over something.

   _____

3. Well, just look at her, she say sort of <u>impish</u>, turning to look at the child, don't she look like a Olivia to you?

   _____

4. I see a wagon and a great big man in black holding a whip. We sure do thank you for your <u>hospitality</u>.

   _____

5. You're a <u>trifling</u> nigger, she say. You git that bucket and bring it back full.

   _____

6. It more like patting another piece of wood. Not a living tree, but a table, a <u>chifferobe</u>.

   _____

7. He say, Oh, me and that mule. She <u>fractious</u>, you know. She went crazy in the field the other day.

   _____

8. I don't know how long this been going on. I don't know when they spect to <u>conclude</u>. I ease back out, wave to the children by the creek, walk back on up home.

   _____

The Color Purple Vocabulary Worksheet Assignment 1 Continued

Part II: Determining the Meaning -- Match the vocabulary words to their dictionary definitions.

____ 1. NOTION   A. Mischievous

____ 2. FRETTING   B. Idea

____ 3. IMPISH   C. Of very little importance; trivial; insignificant

____ 4. HOSPITALITY   D. Worrying

____ 5. TRIFLING   E. Type of furniture having both drawers and space for hanging clothes

____ 6. CHIFFEROBE   F. Inclined to make trouble

____ 7. FRACTIOUS   G. The treatment of guests and strangers in a warm, friendly, generous way

____ 8. CONCLUDE   H. Bring to an end; finish

VOCABULARY ASSIGNMENT 2 *The Color Purple*

Part I: Using Prior Knowledge and Contextual Clues

Below are the sentences in which the vocabulary words appear in the text. Read the sentence. Use any clues you can find in the sentence combined with your prior knowledge, and write what you think the underlined words mean on the lines provided.

1. I <u>scurry</u> bout, doing this, doing that. Mr. _____ sit back by the door gazing here and there.

   _____

2. He talk bout a <u>strumpet</u> in short skirts, smoking cigarettes, drinking gin. Singing for money and taking other women mens.

   _____

3. Harpo and Sofia in the yard now, looking inside the wagon. They faces <u>grim</u>. Who this? Hapro ast. The woman should have been your mammy, he say.

   _____

4. She look me over from head to foot. Then she <u>cackle</u>. Sound like a death rattle.

   _____

5. Well, say Mr. _____ and turn full face on his daddy, All Shug Avery children got the same daddy. I <u>vouch</u> for that.

   _____

6. Course some folks eat cause food taste good to 'em. Then some is <u>gluttons</u>. They love to feel they mouth work.

   _____

7. He <u>rummage</u> through the drawer for a spoon to eat the clabber with.

   _____

8. She not mean, she not <u>spiteful</u>. She don't hold a grudge.

   _____

9. He making a net for <u>seining</u> fish. He look out toward the creek every once in a while and whistle a little tune.

   _____

10. He make right smart money off of her, and she make some too. Plus she gitting strong again and <u>stout</u>.

    _____

The Color Purple Vocabulary Worksheet Assignment 2 Continued

Part II: Determining the Meaning -- Match the vocabulary words to their dictionary definitions.

____ 1. SCURRY   A. Desiring to harm, annoy, frustrate, or humiliate another person

____ 2. STRUMPET   B. People who eat or consumes immoderate amounts of food

____ 3. GRIM   C. Laugh in a shrill, broken manner

____ 4. CACKLE   D. Large fishing net made to hang vertically in the water by weights at the lower edge and floats at the top

____ 5. VOUCH   E. Move quickly or in haste; scamper

____ 6. GLUTTONS   F. Guarantee; certify; attest to

____ 7. RUMMAGE   G. Bulky in figure; heavily built

____ 8. SPITEFUL   H. Uninviting; stern; harsh

____ 9. SEINING   I. Search thoroughly by handling, turning over, or disarranging contents

____ 10. STOUT   J. Prostitute

VOCABULARY ASSIGNMENT 3 *The Color Purple*

Part I: Using Prior Knowledge and Contextual Clues

Below are the sentences in which the vocabulary words appear in the text. Read the sentence. Use any clues you can find in the sentence combined with your prior knowledge, and write what you think the underlined words mean on the lines provided.

1. Bub in and out of jail. If his grandaddy wasn't the colored uncle of the sheriff who look just like Bub, Bub be <u>lynch</u> by now.

   _____

2. Harpo little yellowish girlfriend <u>sulk</u>, hanging over the bar.

   _____

3. She look a little <u>haggard</u> with all Sofia and Harpo children sprung on her at once, but she carry on. Hair a little stringy, slip show, but she carry on.

   _____

4. Angels all in white, white hair and white eyes, look like <u>albinos</u>. God all white too, looking like some stout white man work at the bank.

   _____

5. Mr. _____ rear back in his chair, give Squeak a good look from head to foot. Squeak push her greasy brown hair back from her face. Yeah, say Mr. _____ . I see the <u>resemblance</u>.

   _____

6. I spent fifteen minutes with my children. And she been going on for months bout how ungrateful I is. White folks is a miracle of <u>affliction</u>, say Sofia.

   _____

The Color Purple Vocabulary Worksheet Assignment 3 Continued

Part II: Determining the Meaning -- Match the vocabulary words to their dictionary definitions.

____ 1. LYNCH   A. Remain silent or hold oneself aloof in an ill-humored or offended mood

____ 2. SULK   B. A condition of pain, suffering, or distress

____ 3. HAGGARD   C. People or animals with abnormally pale skin & hair

____ 4. ALBINOS   D. Similarity in appearance

____ 5. RESEMBLANCE   E. Put to death by hanging, by mob action, and without legal authority

____ 6. AFFLICTION   F. Appearing worn and exhausted

VOCABULARY ASSIGNMENT 4 *The Color Purple*

Part I: Using Prior Knowledge and Contextual Clues

Below are the sentences in which the vocabulary words appear in the text. Read the sentence. Use any clues you can find in the sentence combined with your prior knowledge, and write what you think the underlined words mean on the lines provided.

1. I had every one of my babies at home, too. Midwife come, preacher come, a bunch of the good ladies from the church. Just when I hurt so much I don't know my own name, they think a good time to talk bout <u>repent</u>.

   _____

2. They are <u>sanctified</u> religious and very good to me. They live in a nice house next to the church where Samuel preaches, and we spend a lot of time on church business.

   _____

3. But they know a lot more about it than Miss Beasley or any of our other teachers, and besides, they spoke of all the good things they could do for the <u>downtrodden</u> people from whom they sprang.

   _____

4. And now "God" has sent me to watch over them, to protect and cherish them. To <u>lavish</u> all the love I feel for you on them. It is a miracle, isn't it?

   _____

5. They live in such beauty and <u>dignity</u>, Celie. And they give and give and then reach down and give some more, when the name "Africa" is mentioned.

   _____

6. Until you see his eyes you think he's <u>somber</u>, even mean, but he has the most thoughtful and gentle brown eyes.

   _____

7. I studied England on a map, so neat and <u>serene</u>, and I became hopeful in spite of myself that much good for Africa is possible, given hard work and the right frame of mind.

   _____

8. Because the black is so black the eye is simply dazzled, and then there is the shining that seems to come, really, from moonlight, it is so <u>luminous</u>, but their skin glows even in the sun.

   _____

9. Somehow I had not expected to see any white people in Africa, but they are here in <u>droves</u>.

   _____

10. We watched the <u>weary</u> families come home from work, still carrying their cacoa seed buckets in their hands (these double as lunch buckets next day), and sometimes--if they are women--their children on their backs.

The Color Purple Vocabulary Worksheet Assignment 4 Continued

Part II: Determining the Meaning -- Match the vocabulary words to their dictionary definitions.

____ 1. REPENT   A. Quality of being worthy of respect

____ 2. SANCTIFIED   B. Made holy

____ 3. DOWNTRODDEN   C. Feel such sorrow for sin or fault as to change one's life for the better

____ 4. LAVISH   D. Large crowds of human beings

____ 5. DIGNITY   E. Give or bestow in abundance; shower

____ 6. SOMBER   F. Oppressed; trampled upon

____ 7. SERENE   G. Tired

____ 8. LUMINOUS   H. Calm, peaceful, or tranquil

____ 9. DROVES   I. Gloomy, dark, depressing, extremely serious

____ 10. WEARY   J. Radiating or reflecting light; shining; bright

VOCABULARY ASSIGNMENT 5 *The Color Purple*

Part I: Using Prior Knowledge and Contextual Clues

Below are the sentences in which the vocabulary words appear in the text. Read the sentence. Use any clues you can find in the sentence combined with your prior knowledge, and write what you think the underlined words mean on the lines provided.

1. As his greed increased he also began to <u>cultivate</u> the land on which the roofleaf grew.

2. Nobody could remember a time when roofleaf did not exist in <u>overabundant</u> amounts.

3. The women of the village take turns cooking for us, and some are cleaner and more <u>conscientious</u> than others. Olivia gets sick from the food prepared by any of the chief's wives.

4. The women also do not "look in a man's face" as they say. To "look in a man's face" is a <u>brazen</u> thing to do. They look instead at his feet or his knees.

5. Adam and Olivia are nearly as tall as me and doing very well in all their studies. Adam has a special <u>aptitude</u> for figures and it worries Samuel that soon he will have nothing more to teach him in this field, having exhausted his own knowledge.

6. He fell ill with malaria and nothing the healer <u>concocted</u> saved him.

7. She is the most <u>industrious</u> of all Tashi's father's widows, and her fields are praised for their cleanliness, productivity and general attractiveness.

8. Their lives always center around work and their children and other women (since a woman cannot really have a man for a friend without the worse kind of <u>ostracism</u> and gossip).

9. Of course no one in Olinka owns a bicycle, but one of the roadbuilders has one, and all the Olinka men <u>covet</u> it and talk of someday soon purchasing their own.

10. Immediately after understanding the roadbuilders' intentions, the chief set off toward the coast, seeking explanations and <u>reparations</u>.

The Color Purple Vocabulary Worksheet Assignment 5 Continued

Part II: Determining the Meaning -- Match the vocabulary words to their dictionary definitions.

____ 1. CULTIVATE   A. Prepare land for raising crops

____ 2. OVERABUNDANT   B. The act of banishing or excluding

____ 3. CONSCIENTIOUS   C. Amends for wrong or injury done

____ 4. BRAZEN   D. Capability; ability

____ 5. APTITUDE   E. Hard-working

____ 6. CONCOCTED   F. Prepared by mixing ingredients

____ 7. INDUSTRIOUS   G. Defiant; shameless

____ 8. OSTRACISM   H. Meticulously careful; dutiful

____ 9. COVET   I. More than is needed

____ 10. REPARATIONS   J. Wish for longingly

VOCABULARY ASSIGNMENT 6 *The Color Purple*

Part I: Using Prior Knowledge and Contextual Clues

Below are the sentences in which the vocabulary words appear in the text. Read the sentence. Use any clues you can find in the sentence combined with your prior knowledge, and write what you think the underlined words mean on the lines provided.

1. All of her sweet ways went with her. All of her education and a heart <u>intent</u> on doing good. She taught me so much!

   _____

2. They knew she was very sick, but death is not something they think about in relation to their parents or themselves. It was a strange little <u>procession</u>. All of us in our white robes and with our faces painted white.

   _____

3. Only the sky above us do we hold in common. I look at it often as if, somehow, reflected from its <u>immensities</u>, I will one day find myself gazing into your eyes.

   _____

4. Two white men came yesterday and spent a couple of hours strolling about the village, mainly looking at the wells. Such is the <u>innate</u> politeness of the Olinka that they rushed about preparing food for them, though precious little is left, since many of the gardens that flourish at this time of the year have been destroyed.

   _____

5. Two white men came yesterday and spent a couple of hours strolling about the village, mainly looking at the wells. Such is the innate politeness of the Olinka that they rushed about preparing food for them, though precious little is left, since many of the gardens that <u>flourish</u> at this time of the year have been destroyed.

   _____

6. She say, Miss Celie, You better hush. God might hear you . . . . She talk and she talk, trying to budge me way from <u>blasphemy</u>.

   _____

7. You come into the world with God. But only them that search for it inside find it. And sometimes it just <u>manifest</u> itself even if you not looking, or don't know what you looking for.

   _____

8. Well, us talk and talk bout God, but I'm still <u>adrift</u>.

   _____

9. Whenever you trying to pray, and man plop himself on the other end of it, tell him to git lost, say Shug. <u>Conjure</u> up flowers, wind, water, a big rock.

   _____

10. Her bigger children married and gone, and her littlest children mad at her, don't know who she is. Think she act funny, look old and <u>dote</u> on that little white gal she raise.

_____

The Color Purple Vocabulary Worksheet Assignment 6 Continued

Part II: Determining the Meaning -- Match the vocabulary words to their dictionary definitions.

____ 1. INTENT   A. Show excessive fondness or love

____ 2. PROCESSION   B. A group of persons, vehicles, or objects moving along in an orderly, formal manner

____ 3. IMMENSITIES   C. Having the attention sharply focused or fixed on something

____ 4. INNATE   D. Inborn; existing from birth

____ 5. FLOURISH   E. Bring to mind; recall

____ 6. BLASPHEMY   F. Thrive; grow or do well

____ 7. MANIFEST   G. Vastness, boundlessness

____ 8. ADRIFT   H. Without direction or purpose

____ 9. CONJURE   I. Show or demonstrate plainly; reveal

____ 10. DOTE   J. An act of cursing or speaking against God

VOCABULARY ASSIGNMENT 7 *The Color Purple*

Part I: Using Prior Knowledge and Contextual Clues

Below are the sentences in which the vocabulary words appear in the text. Read the sentence. Use any clues you can find in the sentence combined with your prior knowledge, and write what you think the underlined words mean on the lines provided.

1. And as they struggled to put up roofs of this cold, hard, glittery, ugly metal the women raised a deafening <u>ululation</u> of sorrow that echoed off the cavern walls for miles around.

   _____

2. It seems the notion of becoming a missionary struck her one evening she was getting ready for yet another <u>tedious</u> date, and lay in the tub thinking a convent would be better than the castle in which she lived.

   _____

3. And so she cultivated a <u>pious</u> interest in heathens. Fooled her parents. Fooled the Missionary Society, who were so taken with her quick command of languages they sent her to Africa (worst luck!) where she began writing novels about everything under the sun.

   _____

4. My pen name is Jared Hint, she said. In England and even in America, I'm a run-away success. Rich, famous. An eccentric <u>recluse</u> who spends most of his time shooting wild game.

   _____

5. Anyway, she said. When I get to England I'll put a stop to their bloody <u>encroachments</u>. I'll tell them what to do with their bloody road and their bloody rubber plantations and their bloody sunburned but still bloody boring English planters and engineers.

   _____

6. He seemed fond of his grandmother and used to her, but her <u>verbosity</u> produced in him a kind of soberly observant speechlessness.

   _____

7. We made fun of them, but we were <u>riveted</u> on their adventures, and on the ladies' telling of them.

   _____

8. As Aunt Theodosia got closer to the part about her surprise and joy over receiving this medal--which validated her service as an <u>exemplary</u> missionary in the King's colony--DuBoyce's foot began to pat the floor rapidly and uncontrollably.

   _____

9. She and Olivia hugged. But it was a quiet, heavy embrace. Nothing like the <u>boisterous</u>, giggling behavior I expect from them.

   _____

10. Our days are fuller than ever, our <u>sojourn</u> in England already a dream. But all things look brighter because I have a loving soul to share them with.

___

The Color Purple Vocabulary Worksheet Assignment 7 Continued

Part II: Determining the Meaning -- Match the vocabulary words to their dictionary definitions.

____ 1. ULULATION   A. Engrossed; had one's attention held

____ 2. TEDIOUS   B. A person who lives in seclusion or apart from society

____ 3. PIOUS   C. Taking another's possessions or rights gradually or stealthily

____ 4. RECLUSE   D. Wordiness

____ 5. ENCROACHMENTS   E. A temporary stay

____ 6. VERBOSITY   F. Worthy of imitation as a good example

____ 7. RIVETED   G. Tiresome by reason of length, slowness, or dullness

____ 8. EXEMPLARY   H. Loud howling, wailing, or lamenting

____ 9. BOISTEROUS   I. Having or exhibiting religious reverence; devout

____ 10. SOJOURN   J. Rough and noisy; noisily jolly or rowdy

VOCABULARY ASSIGNMENT 8 *The Color Purple*

Part I: Using Prior Knowledge and Contextual Clues

Below are the sentences in which the vocabulary words appear in the text. Read the sentence. Use any clues you can find in the sentence combined with your prior knowledge, and write what you think the underlined words mean on the lines provided.

1. But I think she just so glad to see me. So I <u>preen</u> and pose for her and stuff myself with wonton soup and friend rice.

   _____

2. When I think of them in America I see them as much younger than they appear here. Much more <u>naive</u>.

   _____

3. The worst we have had to <u>endure</u> here is indifference and a certain understandable shallowness in our personal relationships--excluding our relationship with Catherine and Tashi. After all, the Olinka know we can leave, they must stay.

   _____

4. The worst we have had to endure here is <u>indifference</u> and a certain understandable shallowness in our personal relationships--excluding our relationship with Catherine and Tashi. After all, the Olinka know we can leave, they must stay.

   _____

5. And there are male and female warriors who do indeed go on missions of <u>sabotage</u> against the white plantations.

   _____

6. And then, in that honest, <u>forthright</u> way of hers, she gave her reasons. Paramount among them that, because of the scarification marks on her cheeks Americans would look down on her as a savage and shun her, and whatever children she and Adam might have.

   _____

7. And then, in that honest, forthright way of hers, she gave her reasons. <u>Paramount</u> among them that, because of the scarification marks on her cheeks Americans would look down on her as a savage and shun her, and whatever children she and Adam might have.

   _____

8. He asked Tashi to forgive his initial stupid response to the scarification. And to forgive the <u>repugnance</u> he'd felt about the female initiation ceremony.

   _____

9. He assured Tashi that it was she he loved and that in America she would have country, people, parents, sister, husband, brother and lover, and that whatever <u>befell</u> her in America would also be his own choice and his own lot.

   _____

10. All the people down by the drive look up at us. They look at the house. The yard. Shug and Albert's cars. They look round at the fields. Then they <u>commence</u> to walk real slow up the walk to the house.

   _____

The Color Purple Vocabulary Worksheet Assignment 8 Continued

Part II: Determining the Meaning -- Match the vocabulary words to their dictionary definitions.

____ 1. PREEN   A. Direct and straightforward

____ 2. NAIVE   B. Take pride or satisfaction in oneself; gloat

____ 3. ENDURE   C. Happened or occurred

____ 4. INDIFFERENCE   D. Of chief concern or importance

____ 5. SABOTAGE   E. Begin; start

____ 6. FORTHRIGHT   F. Lacking worldly experience and understanding; lacking sophistication

____ 7. PARAMOUNT   G. Attitude of not caring one way or another

____ 8. REPUGNANCE   H. Carry on despite hardships

____ 9. BEFELL   I. Underhanded interference

____ 10. COMMENCE   J. Strong distaste or objection

VOCABULARY ANSWER KEY - *The Color Purple*

	1	2	3	4	5	6	7	8	9
1	B	E	E	C	A	C	H	B	
2	D	J	A	B	I	B	G	F	
3	A	H	F	F	H	G	I	H	
4	G	C	C	E	G	D	B	G	
5	C	F	D	A	D	F	C	I	
6	E	B	B	I	F	J	D	A	
7	F	I		H	E	I	A	D	
8	H	A		J	B	H	F	J	
9		D		D	J	E	J	C	
10		G		G	C	A	E	E	

DAILY LESSONS

LESSON ONE

Objectives
1. To introduce *The Color Purple* unit
2. To distribute books, study questions, and other related materials
3. To preview the vocabulary and study questions for Assignment 1
4. To read Assignment 1
5. To introduce the project assignment for this unit

Activity #1
The first lesson will require several handouts to introduce students to the unit. Prior to the class, create an envelope full of all necessary unit materials for each student, making sure to address each envelope to a student in your class. The goal is to make their unit materials look like a piece of mail, so a stamp of some sort and proper labeling may be a nice addition to each student's letter/packet of resources.

NOTE: If you have time a week before this unit begins, write each of your students a letter and mail it to them. In Lesson One, discuss how getting the letter in the mail made them feel. If you do this, you can skip the letter in the materials packet.

At the start of the unit, distribute envelopes to the students in your class. Ask students not to open them until you give them permission. Before opening the envelopes and beginning to go over the unit, ask students to think about the purposes of a letter. Hold a class discussion on the reasons people write letters, and talk with your students about the reasons people often write both to others and for personal reasons.

Discuss why people don't write as many letters now as they used to (email, instant messenger, texting, etc.). Ask how many times a day your students check their email or phones for messages. Ask why they check so often (Everyone anticipates hearing from friends or family. People used to look forward to the arrival of the mail each day, which would be like only being able to "check your messages" one time each day.)

After the class has talked about the many purposes of letters and writing, explain to students that they will be reading *The Color Purple,* a novel written in a series of letters. You may want to tell students that these letters are not only written as a form of communication, but also as a way of coping and dealing with things in life, almost a method of self-discovery and growth for Celie, the main character.

Activity #2
Ask students to open their envelopes to find the materials they will need for the unit. Direct students to the unit project and spend a few moments going over the project in detail, answering any questions your students may have.

NOTE: If you think your students need more guidance on this project, take time after each reading assignment (perhaps when you do the study questions) to review items from the reading assignment that could/should be included on the character charts. Do as much or as little as you feel your students need. If you choose to do this, make a note on the daily lessons in which the study questions are reviewed for each reading section, so you don't forget.

Activity #3
Direct students to the other materials in their envelopes they will need for the unit. Explain in detail how students are to use these materials.

Study Guides Students should read the study guide questions for each reading assignment prior to beginning the reading assignment to get a feeling for what events and ideas are important in the section they are about to read. After reading the section, students will (as a class or individually) answer the questions to review the important events and ideas from that section of the book. Students should keep the study guides as study materials for the unit test. **Review the study questions for Assignment 1 while you're looking at the study guides.**

Vocabulary Prior to each reading assignment, students will do vocabulary work related to the section of the book they are about to read. Following the completion of the reading of the book, there will be a vocabulary review of all the words used in the vocabulary assignments. Students should keep their vocabulary work as study materials for the unit test. **Do Assignment 1 together orally to show students how to do the vocabulary worksheets.**

Reading Assignment Sheet You need to fill in the reading assignment sheet to let students know by when their reading has to be completed. In the case of *The Color Purple* we have numbered the entries in the order they appear in the book to try to make identification easier. You may want to write in the page numbers of the edition you use for each reading assignment to make sure your students are clear about the assignment. You can either write the assignment sheet up on a side blackboard or bulletin board and leave it there for students to see each day, or you can make copies for each student to have. In either case, you should advise students to become very familiar with the reading assignments so they know what is expected of them.

Extra Activities Center The Unit Resource Materials portion of this LitPlan contains suggestions for an extra library of related books and articles in your classroom as well as crossword and word search puzzles. Make an extra activities center in your room where you will keep these materials for students to use. (Bring the books and articles in from the library and keep several copies of the puzzles on hand.) Explain to students that these materials are available for students to use when they finish reading assignments or other class work early.

Non-fiction Assignment Sheet Explain to students that they each are to read at least one non-fiction piece from the in-class library at some time during the unit. Students will fill out a Non-fiction Assignment Sheet after completing the reading to help you (the teacher) evaluate their reading experiences and to help the students think about and evaluate their own reading experiences.

Books Each school has its own rules and regulations regarding student use of school books. Advise students of the procedures that are normal for your school. Preview the book. Look at the covers, frontmatter, and index.

Activity #4
Tell students that they should read Assignment 1 prior to the next class period. Give them the remainder of this class (if time remains) to complete this assignment.

THE COLOR PURPLE RELATIONSHIP PROJECT *The Color Purple*

PROMPT
Alice Walker creates several memorable characters in her novel *The Color Purple*. Each of these characters interact with others, creating many important relationships. Some relationships are abusive and degrading, while others provide the support needed to endure life's hardships. The goal of this assignment is to analyze the many different relationships between characters and evaluate how characters in this community use these relationships to grow and change throughout the novel.

WHAT TO DO
As a part of this assignment, you have been given character relationship charts for each of the main characters. As you learn more about each character, make notes on this chart about his or her relationships with others. You may want to keep sticky notes or page flags with you while reading so you may easily refer back to pages you need when working on your analysis. After each reading assignment is complete, review your notations and decide what you want to include in your chart.

In your analysis you should pay attention to both major and minor characters in the novel. Just because a character has a small role, doesn't mean he or she didn't significantly influence the life of another character through their relationship. You will also want to pay attention to traditional family relationships like mother, father, son, wife, husband, etc. and analyze whether or not these relationships were as one would expect. Relationships like friend, lover, confidant, etc. should also be included in your project. When analyzing each relationship, include quotes from the novel to illustrate your point. You should also note what each character gives and takes from their relationship, how characters rely on one another, and how characters are changed due to this personal connection. You may also want to note the changes that take place in several of the relationships within the novel.

WHEN YOUR CHARTS ARE DONE
After you have finished reading the book and your chart is completed, you will use the information you have gathered on your chart as a basis for a group discussion about the characters and their relationships.

CHARACTER RELATIONSHIP CHART
The Color Purple
CELIE

Character	Words To Describe The Relationship	Page References	Item That Would Represent The Relationship	Why The Item Is Appropriate
Her Father				
Nettie				
Shug				
Mr. ___				
Sofia				
Olivia & Adam				

CHARACTER RELATIONSHIP CHART
The Color Purple
NETTIE

Character	Words To Describe The Relationship	Page References	Item That Would Represent The Relationship	Why The Item Is Appropriate
Celie				
Her Father				
Mr. ___				
Corrine				
Samuel				
Olivia & Adam				

CHARACTER RELATIONSHIP CHART
The Color Purple
SHUG

Character	Words To Describe The Relationship	Page References	Item That Would Represent The Relationship	Why The Item Is Appropriate
Albert				
Celie				
Mary Agnes (Squeak)				
Grady				
Germaine				
Her Children				

CHARACTER RELATIONSHIP CHART
The Color Purple
SOFIA

Character	Words To Describe The Relationship	Page References	Item That Would Represent The Relationship	Why The Item Is Appropriate
Harpo				
Celie				
Mary Agnes (Squeak)				
Eleanor Jane				
Mayor & His Wife				
Her Children				

CHARACTER RELATIONSHIP CHART
The Color Purple
ALBERT

Character	Words To Describe The Relationship	Page References	Item That Would Represent The Relationship	Why The Item Is Appropriate
Shug				
Celie				
Nettie				
His Children				

CHARACTER RELATIONSHIP CHART
The Color Purple
TASHI

Character	Words To Describe The Relationship	Page References	Item That Would Represent The Relationship	Why The Item Is Appropriate
Her Mother				
Adam				
Olivia				
Samuel/Corrine				
Her Community				

LESSON TWO

Objectives
1. To review main ideas, events, and vocabulary of Assignment 1
2. To create a visual display that will be used during and after reading strategy
3. To analyze gender roles and sexism throughout the novel
4. To preview the vocabulary and study questions for Assignment 2
5. To read Assignment 2

Activity #1
Give students a few minutes to formulate answers to the study guide questions for Assignment 1, and then discuss the answers to the questions in detail. Write the answers on the board or overhead transparency so students can have the correct answers for study purposes.

NOTE: It is a good practice in public speaking and leadership skills for individual students to take charge of leading the discussions of the study questions. Perhaps a different student could go to the front of the class and lead the discussion each day that the study questions are discussed in this unit. Of course, you should guide the discussion when appropriate and try to fill in any gaps students may leave. The study questions could really be handled in a number of different ways, including in small groups with group reports following. Occasionally you may want to use the multiple choice questions as quizzes to check students' reading comprehension. As a short review now and then, students could pair up for the first (or last, if you have time left at the end of a class period) few minutes of class to quiz each other from the study questions. Mix up methods of reviewing the materials and checking comprehension throughout the unit so students don't get bored just answering the questions the same way each day. Variety in methods will also help address the different learning styles of your students. From now on in this unit, the directions will simply say, "Discuss the answers to the study questions in detail as previously directed." You will choose the method of preparation and discussion each day based on what best suits you and your class.

Activity #2
Review the vocabulary answers from the reading. Make sure students write down the correct answers.

Activity #3
After reading Assignment 1, students will have encountered several surprising scenes between men and women in the novel. After this initial reading, students will be able to begin analyzing the gender roles of women and men and the various forms of sexism found throughout the novel.

Divide your class into two groups: boys and girls. Ask the girls to look for scenes in the text that illustrate the expectations of women and their roles in the story. Ask the boys to do the same, analyzing the expectations of men and their roles in the story. Direct students to find specific passages in the text to support their answers. You may want to be sure students are looking at things like education, marriage, family roles, childbearing, raising children, work around the house and on the land, common characteristics, and violence.

As students are working, designate an area on a wall where you can track what the author is saying about gender throughout the unit. You may want to create a compare and contrast chart allowing students to post their findings side by side to compare men and women in the novel.

Once students have had enough time to formulate their answers, come together as a class to discuss their findings. Allow both groups to share how different genders in the novel are expected to behave by society and the opposite sex. Talk about what is tolerated (pay specific attention to the acceptable violence in this reading assignment) and talk about the characteristics seen in each gender.

Encourage students to put ideas on paper and add them to the compare and contrast wall in your room. Tell students that as they read the novel, they will continue to be confronted with sexism and various disputes between the roles and expectations of men and women. Take the time after reviewing the study questions and vocabulary for each section to hold a brief discussion on what can be added to the comparison chart on the wall to aid students in determining what the author is trying to say about gender in her novel.

Activity #4
Review the study questions and vocabulary for Assignment 2 orally together in class. Tell students that they should read Assignment 2 prior to the next class period. Give them the remainder of this class (if time remains) to complete this assignment.

LESSON THREE

Objectives
1. To review main ideas, events, and vocabulary of Assignment 2
2. To analyze the gender roles and sexism in Assignment 2
3. To preview the vocabulary and study questions for Assignment 3
4. To read Assignment 3
5. To evaluate students' oral reading

Activity #1
Discuss the answers to the study guide questions for Assignment 2 as previously directed. Preview the questions for Assignment 3 while students have their study guides out.

Activity #2
Review the vocabulary answers from the reading Assignment 2. Be sure students have the correct answers for study purposes. Instruct students to complete the vocabulary work for Assignment 3.

Activity #3
Continue working on the class assessment of gender roles in the novel as previously described.

Activity #4
Have students read Assignment 3 of *The Color Purple* orally in class. You probably know the best way to get readers with your class; pick students at random, ask for volunteers, or use whatever method works best for your group. If you have not yet completed an oral reading evaluation for your students, this would be a good opportunity to do so. A form is included with this unit for your convenience.

ORAL READING EVALUATION - *The Color Purple*

Name _____ Class____ Date _____

SKILL	EXCELLENT	GOOD	AVERAGE	FAIR	POOR
Fluency	5	4	3	2	1
Clarity	5	4	3	2	1
Audibility	5	4	3	2	1
Pronunciation	5	4	3	2	1
_____	5	4	3	2	1
_____	5	4	3	2	1

Total _____ Grade _____

Comments:

LESSON FOUR

Objectives
1. To have students research and read non-fiction related to the book to help connect the book to real life
2. To broaden students' knowledge about topics related to the book

Activity #1
Take students to the library or media center. With students, brainstorm a list of non-fiction topics that could be related to *The Color Purple*. A short list to get you started is included below.

- African American life following slavery
- Racism
- Sexism
- Domestic Abuse
- Gender roles in a marriage
- How people deal with trauma (such as rape) from childhood as an adult
- The influence of the Bible and the church on how wives must act with their husbands
- Jukejoints and other forms of entertainment in this time period
- Censorship of *The Color Purple*
- The frequency of illegitimate children between white men and black women in the time (how they were viewed, treated, and acknowledged)
- Unnecessary and excessive force when black people are arrested by white officers
- The term "uncle tomming"
- How communities come together to provide strength and support in times of need
- How to overcome emotional hardships in life

Activity #2
Distribute the Non-fiction Assignment Sheet to students. Explain that students should choose a non-fiction topic related to *The Color Purple*. They should read a substantial article related to that topic and complete the Non-fiction Assignment Sheet for that article. Students may use magazines, newspapers, and the Internet as sources.

Activity #3
Bring the class back together and have each student tell what he/she read about.

Note: This activity may require additional class time depending on the level of your students and the amount of time you choose to allow for each student's summary of their topic.

Note: Compiling the Non-fiction Assignment Sheets into a booklet makes a nice follow-up activity and a handy reference for students.

NON-FICTION ASSIGNMENT SHEET
(To be completed after reading the required non-fiction article)

Name _____ Date _____

Title of Non-fiction Read _____

Written By _____ Publication Date _____

I. Factual Summary: Write a short summary of the piece you read.

II. Vocabulary
    1. With which vocabulary words in the piece did you encounter some degree of difficulty?

    2. How did you resolve your lack of understanding with these words?

III. Interpretation: What was the main point the author wanted you to get from reading his work?

IV. Criticism
    1. With which points of the piece did you agree or find easy to accept? Why?

    2. With which points of the piece did you disagree or find difficult to believe? Why?

V. Personal Response: What do you think about this piece? OR How does this piece influence your ideas?

LESSON FIVE

<u>Objectives</u>
1. To review main ideas, events, and vocabulary of Assignment 3
2. To analyze the gender roles and sexism in Assignment 3
3. To examine events in the novel in more detail
4. To preview the vocabulary and study questions for Assignment 4
5. To read Assisgnment 4

<u>Activity #1</u>
Discuss the answers to the study guide questions for reading Assignment 3 as previously directed.

<u>Activity #2</u>
Review the vocabulary answers from reading Assingnemt 3. Be sure students have the correct answers for study purposes.

<u>Activity #3</u>
Continue working on the class assessment of gender roles in the novel as previously described.

<u>Activity #4</u>
Place students in groups of three or four. Ask each group to answer the following questions about their assigned topic.

1. What exactly happened in your assigned event? Provide as many details as possible regarding what occurred.
2. Was what happened fair? Explain why or why not.
3. How did the event impact various characters in the novel?
4. How was the strength of a character or several characters shown in this event?
5. What do you think the author was trying to do in including this event in the novel?

After students have had enough time to fully discuss and answer their questions, jigsaw students so that each new group has one person from each of the previous groups, resulting in each member having worked on a different topic. Ask students to then reexamine their topics and share the findings of their previous group with the new group. After students have shared their previous findings with each other ask them to answer the following question: How does the author use events in the novel to show the strength of characters and develop a strong sense of community through the bonds between characters?

Give students time to answer this question and then pull the class together to discuss the question, using examples brought up in small group discussions. As you guide the discussion, be sure to point out the strong bond within characters and how the strength of the community can provide support to those in need.

A list of suggested topics from the most recent reading assignments is provided below. You may choose to include additional topics depending on the size of your class and the events you want to highlight.

- Celie being forced to marry Mr. _____ and become the mother of his children
- Shug coming to live with Albert and Celie
- Harpo being left by Sofia
- Sofia getting arrested
- Sofia's experience in jail

- Getting Sofia released from jail
- Sofia visiting her children
- Celie sharing with Shug her childhood experiences

Activity #5
Review the study questions and vocabulary for Assignment 4 orally together in class. Tell students that they should read Assignment 4 prior to the next class period. Give them the remainder of this class (if time remains) to complete this assignment.

LESSON SIX

<u>Objectives</u>
1. To review main ideas, events, and vocabulary of Assignment 4
2. To analyze the gender roles and sexism in Assignment 4
3. To enhance students' overall writing ability
4. To bridge connections from the novel to the lives of students
5. To preview the vocabulary and study questions for Assignment 5
6. To read Assignment 5

<u>Activity #1</u>
Discuss the answers to the study guide questions for reading Assignment 4 as previously directed.

<u>Activity #2</u>
Review the vocabulary answers from reading Assignment 4. Be sure students have the correct answers for study purposes.

<u>Activity #3</u>
Continue working on the class assessment of gender roles in the novel as previously described.

<u>Activity #4</u>
In *The Color Purple*, Celie tells a lot of her story through a series of letters to God. In this writing assignment, students will be asked to tell a part of their own story through a personal narrative in the form of a letter. Distribute Writing Assignment 1 and use the attached rubric to give feedback to your students.

<u>Activity #5</u>
Review the study questions and vocabulary for Assignment 5 orally together in class. Tell students that they should read Assignment 5 prior to the next class period. Give them the remainder of this class (if time remains) to complete this assignment.

WRITING ASSIGNMENT #1 *The Color Purple*

PROMPT
Nettie writes to Celie, "I remember one time you said your life made you feel so ashamed you couldn't even talk about it to God, you had to write it, bad as you thought your writing was." Celie uses her letters to God as a way of sorting through what happens to her in life. Through these personal narratives, the reader is able to understand the hardships Celie endures and learn more about her life. Your assignment is to write a short narrative in the form of a letter about something you struggled with or had to endure in your own life, just as Celie writes in her letters to God.

PREWRITING
Think about the difficult times you've experienced in your own life. Make a list of all the difficult times you've endured, jotting down a few details about each event. Your list can include smaller problems like struggling in a class at school, to large problems like dealing with the death of a family member. After compiling your list, select an event you feel comfortable writing about. Make sure the event you select is one you remember clearly so you can include specific details in your writing.

DRAFTING
Begin your writing assignment by selecting someone to address your letter to. Remember, this is a personal narrative, so it should be written in first person point of view. The beginning of your letter should set the scene for the reader, giving information on your age, the location of the event, and other necessary details for the reader to later understand your problem.

The body of your letter should provide details about the struggle you endured. Celie's readers are able to sympathize with her because of the great detail she uses in her writing. Try to include your emotions, your thoughts, and any dialogue or reactions from those around you.

To conclude your letter, think about how you found the strength to resolve the hardship. Talk about who in your life gave you the support you needed, or how you found the strength on your own. If the hardship is ongoing, talk about what you are currently doing to deal with it. At the end of your letter, remember to sign your name.

PROMPT
When you finish the rough draft of your letter, ask a student who sits near you to read it. After reading your rough draft, he/she should tell you what he/she liked best about your work, which parts were difficult to understand, and ways in which your work could be improved. Reread your paper considering your critic's comments, and make the corrections you think are necessary.

PROOFREADING
Do a final proofreading of your paper double-checking your grammar, spelling, organization, and the clarity of your ideas.

WRITING EVALUATION FORM *The Color Purple*

Name_____ Date_____

Writing Assignment #_____ Grade_____

Circle One For Each Item:

Beginning:	excellent	good	fair	poor
Middle:	excellent	good	fair	poor
End:	excellent	good	fair	poor
Grammar:	excellent	good	fair	poor
Spelling:	excellent	good	fair	poor
Punctuation:	excellent	good	fair	poor
Legibility:	excellent	good	fair	poor
Creativity:	excellent	good	fair	poor
_____:	excellent	good	fair	poor
_____:	excellent	good	fair	poor
_____:	excellent	good	fair	poor

Strengths:

Weaknesses:

Comments/Suggestions

LESSON SEVEN

Objectives
1. To review main ideas, events, and vocabulary of Assignment 5
2. To analyze the gender roles and sexism in Assignment 5
3. To analyze events in the novel
4. To bridge connections from the novel to the lives of students
5. To preview the vocabulary and study questions for Assignment 6

Activity #1
Discuss the answers to the study guide questions for reading Assignment 5 as previously directed.

Activity #2
Review the vocabulary answers from reading Assignment 5. Be sure students have the correct answers for study purposes.

Activity #3
Continue working on the class assessment of gender roles in the novel as previously described.

Activity #4
While reading her letters from Nettie, Celie is able to learn a lot about the Olinka culture. In many ways, this culture that seems so foreign, is remarkably similar to the culture in which Celie lives. Place students in small groups and instruct them to take out their novels. Distribute the Venn Diagram. Explain to students they should label the first circle "Celie's Life", the second cirlce "Olinka Culture", and the third circle "Present Day." Ask students to use their novels to compare and contrast the community Celie lives in with the Olinka community and the community in which you and your students live. As you circulate the classroom, try to guide students to think about topics like gender roles and expectations, religion, education, community, marriage, and family. When students have completed their Venn Diagram, ask them to review their information and write a brief statement at the bottom of their paper summarizing their findings. If class time permits, allow students to reflect on these three cultures as a class and share their discoveries with each other.

Note: If your students are unfamiliar with Venn Diagrams, you may need to spend a few minutes at the start of class modeling how to use this graphic organizer as a method of comparing and contrasting different items.

Activity #5
Review the study questions and vocabulary for Assignment 6 orally together in class. Tell students that they should read Assignment 6 prior to the next class period.

Comparing Three Things

Item 1: _____   Item 2: _____

Item 3: _____

Summary: _____
_____
_____
_____

LESSON EIGHT

<u>Objectives</u>
1. To review main ideas, events, and vocabulary of Assignment 6
2. To analyze the gender roles and sexism in Assignment 6
3. To examine the climax of the novel in more detail

<u>Activity #1</u>
Discuss the answers to the study guide questions for reading Assignment 6 as previously directed.

<u>Activity #2</u>
Review the vocabulary answers from reading Assignment 6. Be sure students have the correct answers for study purposes.

<u>Activity #3</u>
Continue working on the class assessment of gender roles in the novel as previously described.

<u>Activity #4</u>
In Assignment 6, students encountered the climax of the novel--Celie's ability to realize who she is and stand up to someone who is putting her down. This reading assignment signifies great growth and change in both Celie's view of God and her self confidence. In this activity, students will be asked to examine Celie's growth and analyze the change that takes place in this portion of the novel. Begin by dividing students into small groups. Assign each of these groups one of two topics: Celie's self discovery and new confidence or Celie's realizations about God. Ask students to look for passages in the text that correlate with their assigned topic. While students are searching for topics to illustrate Celie's growth, distribute small squares of colored construction paper. After giving students a chance to brainstorm in small groups and chart her development in this reading assignment, bring the class back together to give additional instructions.

Briefly talk to your students about the symbol of the quilt in the novel. Talk to students about what quilting symbolizes, urging them to see that in the process of quilting, several diverse pieces come together to make one unified piece. Talk to students about how this symbol is used in the text and then tell them they will be creating a quilt themselves. Instruct students to use the colorful squares of construction paper to show Celie's growth at this point in the novel. They should add quotes from the text, illustrations, and their own descriptions to show the change in Celie's view of God and the change in her view of herself. Once students have finished their quilt pieces, come together as a class to share the pieces and generate a more in-depth discussion about the climax of the novel. You can later use yarn to tie the quilt pieces together to create an authentic looking quilt to display in your classroom.

LESSON NINE

Objectives
1. To give students the opportunity to practice writing to persuade
2. To improve students' overall writing ability
3. To preview the vocabulary and study questions for Assignment 7
4. To read Assignment 7

Activity #1
Review the study questions and vocabulary for Assignment 7 orally together in class. Tell students that they should read Assignment 7 prior to the next class period.

Activity #2
It takes several years for Celie to realize her true worth and stand up for herself while Albert is criticizing her. Even though she had people like Nettie, Sofia, and Shug to encourage her and improve her self confidence, it still takes Celie a long time to put an end to Albert's abuse. In this writing assignment, students will be writing to persuade a friend in a similar situation to realize their full potential and self worth. Distribute Writing Assignment 2 and discuss the directions in detail. Give students the remaining class time to work on this assignment. Inform students when this writing assignment is due.

WRITING ASSIGNMENT #2 *The Color Purple*

PROMPT
It takes Celie several years of abuse from her stepfather, Albert, and his children to finally stand up for herself and believe her life has value. With the help of Nettie, Sofia, and Shug, Celie is able to discover herself and realize her own strength. Your assignment is to write to persuade someone with low self-esteem who is in a bad situation to find his or her own strength, just like Celie does when she stands us to Albert.

PREWRITING
Think about people you know, have read about, or seen on TV that have low self-esteem. Devise a short list of harmful situations these people endure due to their lack of inner strength. Next, come up with several ways to help someone realize his or her true worth. You may want to think about ways Nettie, Sofia, and Shug provide support for Celie, and pay attention to other female characters in the novel who show strength and serve as a role model for Celie.

DRAFTING
This essay should be written in first person and should be speaking directly to who you are trying to help. This person can be real or made up, as long as it is clear to the reader what type of negative situation this person is in because of his or her low self-esteem and lack of inner strength.

After pointing out the severity of the situation to the person you are trying to help, use the body of your writing to talk about how this person can find inner strength to ultimately change his or her life. Use the ideas you generated in your prewriting to help you convince this person to see his or her own value in life and make a change for a better life. You may want to use examples from the text to help make your point.

Your conclusion should summarize the reasons why this person needs to change his or her life and offer a few last words of advice to leave the reader with a lasting impact.

PROMPT
When you finish the rough draft of your composition, ask a student who sits near you to read it. After reading your rough draft, he/she should tell you what he/she liked best about your work, which parts were difficult to understand, and ways in which your work could be improved. Reread your paper considering your critic's comments, and make the corrections you think are necessary. Ask your classmate what he/she thought of each of the characters/events you chose for your assignment.

PROOFREADING
Do a final proofreading of your paper double-checking your grammar, spelling, organization, and the clarity of your ideas.

LESSON TEN

<u>Objectives</u>
To bring ideas from the book into real life

<u>Activity</u>
This day has been set aside for a guest speaker. Invite one or more of the following people from your community to speak to your class:

- A missionary who has worked overseas
- A counselor for abused children
- A police officer who deals with domestic violence
- Someone from the NAACP to speak about racism
- Someone from a women's advocacy group to talk about the gender gap
- A successful black business owner
- Professor of cultural studies to discuss the female initiation and scarification ceremonies that take place in other parts of the world
- Professor of religious studies to discuss the impact of religion on society
- A community leader to talk about how people come together in the community to provide support for others

Divide your class time according to how many speakers you're able to acquire. Remember to allow time for students to ask questions. Let each speaker know how much time he/she will have for the presentation. Allow for time at the end of the class for students to make connections with what they have learned from the speakers with what they have read in *The Color Purple*.

Follow Up: Be sure you and your students write thank you notes to each of your guests. At the very least, get a thank you card for each guest and have each of your students sign it (with any personal responses, if there is room).

LESSON ELEVEN

Objectives
1. To review the main ideas, events, and vocabulary of Assignment 7
2. To analyze the gender roles and sexism in Assignment 7
3. To broaden students' knowledge on topics discussed in the novel
4. To provide students with the background knowledge needed to understand events in the novel
5. To preview the vocabulary and study questions for Assignment 8
6. To read Assignment 8

Activity #1
Discuss the answers to the study questions for reading Assignment 7 as previously directed.

Activity #2
Review the vocabulary answers from reading Assignment 7. Be sure students have the correct answers for study purposes.

Activity #3
Continue working on the class assessment of gender roles in the novel as previously directed.

Activity #4
The Color Purple introduces students to several new concepts and practices through Nettie's letters from the Olinka village. Today has been set aside for you to explore these new practices with your students to help them better understand what is taking place in the village from which Nettie writes.

Much of what Nettie tells Celie about is the growing conflict between the Olinka people and the rubber factory that has forced them off their land. Talk to your students about imperialism and the cultivation of land in Africa for resources used throughout the world. Rubber, diamonds, oil, coffee, and cocoa are the most common resources taken from Africa. Many of these resources are not "conflict-free" and do not follow international labor laws for adults and children.
The BBC has a wealth of information and videos on these topics on their website, and a simple google search will uncover more information for you to share with your students. Checking out a projector and laptop would be the best way to cover these topics, but you can also use non-fiction articles or informational videos, depending on what resources are available to you at the time you teach this LitPlan. As you are covering these topics with your students, try to bridge a connection between the novel and what is taking place in real life. Talk to your students about people being forced off their land to work in grueling conditions for little money. Draw a link between the school-age boys in the Olinka village being put to work with practices taking place in something current, like cocoa plantations. Try to push your students to understand that much of what they enjoy now, comes for a price as seen in the novel. Most students have not had previous exposure to the idea of taking resources and moving people from their land, so try to provide them with enough information to fully understand what is happening to the Olinka people in the novel.

Nettie also writes to Celie about the customs of the Olinka people. While the female initiation ceremony and the scarification ritual sound backwards to most Americans, Tashi points out that it's her way of keeping the Olinka culture alive. Use today to educate your students on the purposes of some of these rituals. The National Geographic website has several videos from their hit TV show *Taboo*. This show explores customs from cultures all over the world and tries to explain the pride many cultures take in these rituals, while explaining their purpose. The National Geographic magazine would also be a great place to look for non-fiction articles to read with your students on this topic. Students are probably not familiar with the female initiation ceremony Tashi takes part in. If you feel comfortable with this topic, talk to your students about the female circumcision process Tashi participates in. Alice Walker has another book called *Possessing the Secret of Joy* which tells the story of Tashi, Adam, and Olivia from their point of view. Excerpts from this novel could be used to read from Tashi's point of view what happened to her when she underwent this rite of passage for women and how she made the decision to move forward with such a controversial ritual. There is also plenty of information available on the Internet that looks at this topic from a both the view of the culture practicing this procedure, and from contemporary medical professionals examining the dangers.

Activity #5
Review the study questions and vocabulary for Assignment 8 orally together in class. Tell students that they should read Assignment 8 prior to the next class.

LESSON TWELVE

Objectives
1. To review main ideas, events, and vocabulary of Assignment 8
2. To analyze the gender roles and sexism in Assignment 8
3. To evaluate each character's growth throughout the novel

Activity #1
Discuss the answers to the study guide questions for reading Assignment 8 as previously directed.

Activity #2
Review the vocabulary answers from reading Assignment. Be sure students have the correct answers for study purposes.

Activity #3
Continue working on the class assessment of gender roles in the novel as previously described.

Activity #4
Break your class down into groups either by assigning each student a character group or allowing students to choose the character group (one group for each main character chart).

Students should compare their notes about their character's relationships with other characters in the book. Discuss references, objects selected to represent the relationships, and what the relationships meant to the people involved.

Students should come to a consensus about the relationships their character has with others in the novel--a description of each relationship, the best thing that would symbolize each relationship, and a summary of what the character learns, how he/she changes, and/or what we learn about the character from each relationship. Finally they should draw conclusions about how and why the character changed throughout the story.

After students have had time to discuss and come to a consensus, each group should report about its discussions to lead a whole class discussion about individual characters' relationships.

Activity #5
After all groups have reported and the class has discussed all of the individual characters, look at all of the characters as a whole. Which characters are successful? Which characters have good relationships? What leads to good relationships? Compare generations: Celie & Nettie's mother and father as compared to the relationships in Celie and Nettie's generation--and that compared to Adam and Olivia's generation. Which children were cared for, and which were not? Did that affect the outcome of their relationships and their lives? What larger points can be drawn from the book looking at the outcomes of the relationships over generations? Thoroughly discuss the larger implications of the relationships students have investigated.

LESSON THIRTEEN

<u>Objectives</u>
To explore a major theme in the novel

<u>Activity</u>
Throughout the novel students have been working on a visual display to compare and contrast men and women's roles and expectations in the novel. At this point, students should have added several events from the story to help depict how men and women are treated in the book. Place the following quote on the board and ask students to reflect on its meaning:

"Mr. _____ ast me the other day what it is I love so much bout Shug. He say he love her style. He say to tell the truth, Shug act more manly than most men. I mean she upright, honest. Speak her mind and the devil take the hindmost, he say. You know Shug will fight, he say. Just like Sofia. She bound to live her life and her herself no matter what. Mr. _____ think all this is stuff men do. But Harpo not like this, I tell him. You not like this. What Shug got is womanly to it seem like to me. Specially since she and Sofia the ones got it. Sofia and Shug not like men, he say, but they not like women either. You mean they not like you or me."

Hold a brief class discussion about the meaning of the quote. Next, transition your discussion to talking about what Alice Walker was trying to say about gender roles in her novel. You may want to set up a debate in your classroom, or have students put their desks in a circle to have a more open forum for discussion. Ask students to use specific examples from their compare and contrast display to help make their points about gender expectations and realities in the novel. Since this is a major theme in the story, try to get students to think about the larger picture and really analyze Walker's words to find the message she was trying to convey. If class time permits, you may also want to transition the discussion to talk about the women in the novel having a strong sense of community, coming together to provide strength in hard times. Be sure to ask students to point out examples and analyze events from both Celie's life and Nettie's life while living in the Olinka village.

LESSON FOURTEEN

Objectives
1. To give students the opportunity to practice writing to inform
2. To improve students' overall writing ability

Activity

Distribute the RAFT writing assignment to students. Explain that the purpose of this assignment is to write to inform. Tell students that they should select one of the scenarios listed for their third writing assignment. Explain that the "R" stands for the role they will take, or the point of view they are writing from; the "A" stands for the audience they are writing to; the "F" stands for the format of their writing; and the "T" stands for the topic or task. Quickly go over the different scenarios available to them and give the remaining time for students to complete the assignment.

Note: While students complete this writing assignment, call individuals up for writing conferences on the past two writing assignments. Use the evaluation form to guide you in your conference.

The Color Purple Writing Assignment – RAFT

Directions: Select one of the following writing situations to use as the topic for your essay.

| Role
The voice you take on as a writer; this is the perspective you are writing from | Audience
Who you are writing to; this is the person that will be reading what you write | Format
The form your writing will take; this is the type of writing you will complete | Topic/Task
Your purpose for writing; this is the content or reason for your writing assignment |
|---|---|---|---|
| Missionary | Friends back home | Letter | Challenges of being a missionary in a strange culture |
| Black Business Owner in Celie's town | The community | Editorial in a newspaper | The difficulties in running a business in a racist town |
| Preacher in Celie's town | The congregation | Sermon | The changing way people are experiencing and connecting with God |
| Second Wife of a man with three children in Celie's town | Your self | Diary Entry | Expectations of your husband and your role in the family and community |
| Husband of three children in Celie's town | Son | How-to guide | Teaching your son how to run a household and live life |
| Someone who has endured hard times | Others who have endured hard times | Poem | Finding inner strength to continue on even through challenging times |
| A young Olinka female | Other Olinka teens | Speech | Why it is important to go through the scarification ceremony and female initiation ceremony |

WRITING ASSIGNMENT #3 *The Color Purple*

PROMPT
Select one of the scenarios listed on the RAFT writing assignment for the topic of your essay. The role is the point of view from which you are writing, the audience is to whom you are writing, the format is the type of writing you are doing, and the topic/task is the actual information you are writing about.

PREWRITING
Once you have selected your writing scenario, begin to brainstorm ideas. Remember to think about the role you are writing from and the topic you are writing about. Use your book, notes from the speaker, and notes from the non-fiction articles to help you with your support.

DRAFTING
Write an introductory paragraph that allows the reader to know the role you have assumed and the audience to whom you are writing. Give a general overview of the points you will make in the body paragraphs of your writing. Use the format of your writing to guide you on how to begin (speech would begin with a little about yourself, letter begins with Dear _____, etc).

In the body paragraphs, give the details of your topic. Use information from the novel, the speaker, and the non-fiction article you read to help provide support. Be sure to reread the topic/task you are writing on and be sure to cover all portions listed there.

In your conclusion paragraph, summarize your main points and conclude the writing assignment. For unity with your writing, you may want to tie in your role and audience once again.

PROMPT
When you finish the rough draft of your composition, ask a student who sits near you to read it. After reading your rough draft, he/she should tell you what he/she liked best about your work, which parts were difficult to understand, and ways in which your work could be improved. Reread your paper considering your critic's comments, and make the corrections you think are necessary. Ask your classmate what he/she thought of each of the characters/events you chose for your assignment.

PROOFREADING
Do a final proofreading of your paper double-checking your grammar, spelling, organization, and the clarity of your ideas.

LESSON FIFTEEN

Objectives

1. To help students organize the events of the story and the feelings and experiences of each character
2. To discuss the novel on a deeper than direct-recall level
3. To prepare students for questions and topics covered on the test
4. To allow students to make personal connections with the text

Activity #1

Choose the questions from the Extra Discussion Questions/Writing Assignments which seem most appropriate for your students. A class discussion of these questions is most effective if students have been given the opportunity to formulate answers to the questions prior to the discussion. To this end, you may either have all the students formulate answers to all the questions, divide your class into groups and assign one or more questions to each group, or you could assign one question to each student in your class. The option you choose will make a difference in the amount of class time needed for this activity.

Note: The use of graphic organizers may be helpful to students in preparing their answers. Encourage them to use any diagrams or graphics that they feel are necessary.

EXTRA DISCUSSION QUESTIONS/WRITING ASSIGNMENTS *The Color Purple*

<u>Interpretive</u>
1. Describe the author's writing style.
2. How does the point of view enhance the novel?
3. What genre does the story fall under?
4. What are the main conflicts in the story? Describe each fully.
5. What is the setting, and what does it add to the story?

<u>Critical</u>
6. How does Celie react when she gives birth to her first child? Why does she say, "you could have knock me over with a feather."
7. In what ways does Celie make sacrifices for Nettie while still living at home?
8. Compare and contrast the different ways Celie's father views her and her sister.
9. How does Mr. _____ handle his children? How does this effect Celie?
10. Why does Mr. _____ beat Celie? How does she endure these severe beatings?
11. How does Celie react when she hears about Shug Avery before they meet? How does Mr. _____ act when Shug comes to perform in town for the short weekend?
12. Compare and contrast Harpo and his father.
13. How does Celie feel about Mr. _____'s children? How do other people perceive how she feels about his children?
14. How does Celie react when her husband's girlfriend comes to stay at their house? How do others think she should act? Why is there such a difference in the way she acts with the way others expect her to act?
15. How does Celie's relationship with her husband change while Shug is staying with them?
16. Why does Sofia leave Harpo? How has he changed over the course of their marriage?
17. Describe Celie's struggle with the feelings she is beginning to have for Shug.
18. Do the men have a double standard when it comes to women in the jukejoint? Why do they think it is scandalous for their wives and other women family members to go to the jukejoint, when they see nothing wrong with their girlfriends and Shug frequenting this type of place?
19. How does Sofia get by while in prison? What does this do to her character?
20. How do the characters in the novel use their illegitimate connections with white people? Why do you think the white people are so happy to oblige?
21. What does Sofia's boyfriend, the prizefighter, mean when he says the plan to get Sofia out of jail "sound mighty much like some ole uncle Tomming to me."?
22. How does Squeak change after she is raped by the warden?
23. Why does Miz Millie feel she is being kind and generous to the black people she knows? How do the black people feel about this treatment?
24. Miz Millie has no problem driving with Sofia in the front seat as she is teaching her how to drive her new car. Why does she have a problem with Sofia riding in the front seat when they are going somewhere?
25. Compare and contrast how Miz Millie and Sofia view her first visit home to see her children after being gone several years.
26. How do Albert and Celie react when they see Shug and Grady? Why does Shug give up on going after Albert?
27. Why does Shug get buddy-buddy with Albert even though she is married?

28. Compare and contrast the Albert Shug fell in love with many years ago with the Albert Celie is married to now.
29. How did Shug treat Albert's first wife? Why did she treat her this way, and later why did she treat Celie the way she did? How does she feel about it all these years later?
30. What does Nettie mean when she says, "In the short time we've been together they've been like family to me. Like family might have been, I mean."?
31. How does Nettie's story weave into Sofia's story in the novel?
32. How does Nettie's perception of colored people and white people change as she leaves her home town and heads out into the world?
33. Describe the missionary situation in Africa. Which countries have people serving there, and what race are they? How do they identify with the African people?
34. How are the white people in England different than the white people in the South in regards to how they treat black people?
35. What surprises Nettie when she arrives in Africa?
36. How does Nettie feel the first time she saw the African coast? Why did she feel this way?
37. How does Shug convince Celie to not kill Mr. _____ after discovering all the letters he hid from her over the years?
38. How does the relationship between Celie and Shug change as they are reading the letters from Nettie?
39. What emotions does Celie feel when she thinks about her children?
40. Describe the roles of men and women in the Olinka society. How do they differ from the roles of men and women in the society Celie lives in? How are they the same?
41. In what ways do the Olinka people value the missionaries? In what ways do they resent the missionaries?
42. Why do the Olinka people tell Olivia she will be the wife of a chief? Do they mean this as a compliment or an insult? How does Olivia view this statement?
43. How do Olivia and Adam like growing up in Africa instead of the States? Describe their reactions to the Olinka people. What do they like? What do they dislike?
44. Describe Corrine's growing suspicions and resentment toward Nettie. Why does she feel this way?
45. What does Nettie mean when she says, "Aha. Tashi knows she is learning a way of life she will never live."?
46. How do the Olinka people view Nettie, a single woman on her own? How does this view effect Nettie?
47. Compare and contrast the story Samuel was told about Adam and Olivia with the truth that Nettie knows. What surprises do both Nettie and Samuel receive?
48. How does Celie's Pa react when Celie and Shug show up for a visit?
49. How does Celie benefit from visiting her Pa after finding out who he really is?
50. Celie's Pa says, "The trouble with our people is as soon as they got out of slavery they didn't want to give the white man nothing else. But the fact is, you got to give 'em something. Either your money, your land, your woman or your ass." What does he mean by this statement? How has he found success by following his own advice?
51. Why did Corrine have such a difficult time believing she had once met Olivia and Adam's real mother? What happens once she finally knows and accepts the truth about her children?
52. Describe Shug's view of God and how He fits into life.

53. What does Shug mean when she says, "You have to git man off your eyeball, before you can see anything a'tall. Man corrupt everything, say Shug. He on your box of grits, in your head, and all over the radio. He try to make you think he everywhere. Soon as you think he everywhere, you think he God. But he ain't."?
54. Harpo doesn't see the difference in calling Mary Agnes by her real name or calling her by her nickname, Squeak. How are the two names different to Mary Agnes? Why is it difficult for Harpo to see the difference even once she explains it to him?
55. How does Celie change once she begins to see God in a new light?
56. Compare and contrast what Albert means when he says, "Look at you. You black, you pore, you ugly, you a woman. Goddam, he say, you nothing at all," with what Celie means when she says, "I'm pore, I'm black, I may be ugly and can't cook, a voice say to everything listening. But I'm here."
57. As Celie leaves she curses Albert. Where does this curse come from? Whose words are these? Use evidence from the text to support your answer.
58. How does Mr. _____ react when he sees Celie for the first time after she left him? How does Celie react after speaking with her husband?
59. Compare and contrast the philosophy of the white missionary, Doris Baines, with that of Samuel and Nettie.
60. Samuel says, "the Olinka resented us, but I wouldn't see it. But they do, you know." Nettie says in return, "No, I said, it isn't resentment, exactly. It really is indifference." Why does Samuel think the Olinka resent them? What does Nettie mean when she says she thinks their treatment is more like indifference?
61. Why does Tashi decide to scar her face and go through with female circumcision? How do her views on these tribal traditions vary from the views of Adam and Olivia?
62. What does Celie mean when she says, "My heart hurt so much I can't believe it. How can it keep beating, feeling like this? But I'm a woman."?
63. Mr. _____ and Celie begin to develop a relationship once Celie has moved into her own home and established herself in the pants business. What does Mr. _____ do to reconcile their relationship? What does he learn about Celie's feelings for men?
64. What worries does Nettie have for Adam and Olivia once they return to the United States? How will being an educated and opinionated black person in Africa differ from being this same person in America?
65. Most people would say Celie would be justified in hating Mr. _____ for the way he treated her during their marriage. However, Celie doesn't hate him. Why doesn't she hate him? How is she able to develop a friendship with him?
66. Compare and contrast how Shug and Albert regarded Annie Julia with the way they regarded Celie. Why did Shug and Albert act so differently between the two wives?
67. Celie explains to Albert that the men in Africa wear robes similar to dresses to beat the heat and men also sew in Africa. Albert is shocked men would be so similar to women and Celie responds by saying, "They not so backward as mens here." How is this statement an example of irony?
68. In entry 87 Celie and Albert talk about the Olinka view of religion and how their story of creation is intertwined with Christianity. Reread this section and determine what point the author is trying to make.
69. Why does Celie address many of her letters to God?
70. Describe how second wives are treated by their husbands in the novel. What is their purpose? How do their husbands view them?
71. Who does Celie rely on to help her get through the terrible things that continue to happen to her?

72. How does Celie feel about standing up for herself and fighting back against others who don't treat her properly? How does this change over the course of the novel? Use evidence from the text to support your answer.
73. What keeps Celie's anger under control? What prevents her from getting mad, despite all that happens to her?
74. What is Celie's first impression of Shug? How does that change over time?
75. What is Shug's first impression of Celie? How does that change over time?
76. Albert is obviously attracted to Shug, who is an outspoken woman who speaks her mind and does as she pleases. If he is attracted to this type of woman, why does he beat Celie into submission and never let her say anything she is thinking?
77. How does Celie grow and change as a result of Shug's influence?
78. Why do people look down on Shug's lifestyle?
79. The characters in the novel have a lot to be angry about. Several characters treat each other inappropriately and without respect. However, they are usually able to forgive each other quickly, understanding the hardships they too are enduring. What does this say about the characters in the novel? What does this say about the life of black people in this time? Use specific examples from the novel to support your answer.
80. How does Celie's view of God change over the course of the novel?
81. Nettie says, "God is different to us now, after all these years in Africa. More spirit than ever before, and more internal. Most people think he has to look like something or someone--a roofleaf or Christ--but we don't. And not being tied to what God looks like, frees us." How does this view of God correlate with the view Shug shares with Celie? How does this view of God help various characters in the novel?
82. How has Mr. _____ changed and grown over the course of the novel?
83. What is the author trying to say about gender roles throughout the novel? Use examples from the text to support your answer.
84. What is the significance of the title of the novel?
85. Why does Celie refer to her husband as Mr. _____ throughout the novel? Why does the author choose to never have Celie use his real name?
86. What does Celie learn over the course of the novel? How does she grow and change as a result of events that take place in her life? Support your answer with details from the text.
87. Describe the relationship between Celie and Shug. How does in grow and change over the course of the novel? What does each character give and take from that relationship? How does it help both Celie and Shug?
88. Sofia put it best when she said, "Everybody learn something in life." Several characters change over the course of the novel, learning from the events that take place in their lives. Select three characters from the novel and outline how they change as a result of events in the story.

Critical/Personal Response

89. What are your first impressions of Sofia? How does she treat Mr. _____ and Harpo? What does this reveal about her character?
90. Sofia is in charge of the household when it comes to her marriage to Harpo, yet Mr. _____ is in charge of the household in his marriage to Celie. Why are these two households so different? Which household do you think has a healthier relationship? Explain your answer.
91. Celie looks at death as a reward for her actions and obedience while on earth. Is it odd for her to feel this way? Can you relate to this feeling?

92. Celie admits that she has never been turned on by a man. Celie is also realizing that she is attracted to Shug. Why do you think she has trouble being attracted to men? Why do you think she is developing an attraction to Shug?

93. Do you think the police treated Sofia any differently when they arrested her due to her race? Explain your answer using details from the text.

94. How does Celie finally confront what happened between her and her father as a child? How do you think she feels finally telling someone other than God? How do you deal with difficult things that have happened to you in your life?

95. Nettie says, "And it is easy to forget that Africa's 'hard times' were made harder by them." What does she mean by this statement? Do you agree or disagree with what she is saying? Do you think the world has made it easy or difficult for Africa now to get out of the trouble it's in? Explain your answer.

96. The Olinka people say, "A girl is nothing to herself; only to her husband can she become something." Do you think this same statement is true for the characters in the novel living in the States? Explain your answer using details about specific characters.

97. Describe the relationship between the many wives of an Olinka man. How would you think they would regard each other? How do they actually regard each other? What type of relationship do the men have with their wives? What do you think of this behavior?

98. Celie gets teased by her coworkers about the way she talks. They think her dialect makes other people assume she is dumb. Do you think the way Celie speaks effects other people's perceptions of her? Do you think the same is true for the people in the society you live in? Explain your answer.

99. The Olinka people are first forced to pay rent on their own land and are later required to leave their buildings and move to a barren piece of land. Why don't they fight back? What can these people do? Do you think this type of treatment is fair? Does this type of treatment still occur today?

100. Samuel admits he used the think Africans were "savages, they were bumbling, incpt savages." How does this view compare to what Samuel has experienced in his time in Africa learning about the Olinka culture? Do you think people now still view Africans the same way? Is this a correct way of thinking? Explain your answer.

101. Celie discovers that the house, land, and dry goods store have actually belonged to her and Nettie since their mother's death when they were young. How does she react to this news? How would you have reacted if you were in her position?

102. Mr. _____ and Celie sit talking about the characteristics of men and women. Mr. _____ seems to think strong women resemble men, since women are the weaker sex. Celie disagrees, pointing out that Shug and Sofia are much stronger people than Harpo and his father, making strength a womanly trait. Which character do you think is correct? Why?

103. Shug and Germaine go to the State Department to try and find out more about Nettie's ship sinking, however, they are not given any information about what happened. Celie tells Albert, "It's a big war. So much going on. One ship lost feel like nothing, I guess." Do you think this attitude towards small numbers of casualties during war is still the same today? Explain why or why not.

104. At the end of the novel Celie and Nettie are reunited. Describe how you would feel if you were in Celie's situation at the end of the story.

Personal Response

105. Celie is a timid person who doesn't stand up to others. Compare and contrast Celie's personality to your own.

106. Celie says, "First time I think about the world. What the world got to do with anything, I think." How often do you think about the world and your place in it? Do you think the rest of the world has anything to do with you life? Explain your answer.

107. Nettie says about her teacher, "But one thing I do thank her for, for teaching me to learn for myself, by reading and studying and writing a clear hand. And for keeping alive in me somehow the desire to *know*." Do you feel this same way about your own education? Explain why or why not.

108. Celie is outraged that Mr. _____ hid her sister's letters over the years and fights the strong desire to kill him. If you were in her situation, what would you do?

109. The Olinka people say, "A girl is nothing to herself; only to her husband can she become something." How would you respond if someone told you this now? Why would you feel that way?

110. Nettie writes to Celie, "There is so much we don't understand. And so much unhappiness comes because of that." Do you agree or disagree with this statement? Use examples from your own life to support your answer.

111. Shug and Celie have very different views about who God is and how religion fits into their lives. What are your own personal views about God? What role does religion play in your life?

112. Celie relies on God to help her through the terrible experiences she has in life. What do you rely on to help you get through challenging times?

113. Several characters in the novel are able to easily forgive others for treating them poorly, understanding that they too are enduring hard time. How do you forgive others? What challenges do you have with forgiving? What positive reasons do you see for understanding others and trying to forgive them?

114. What portions of the book were hard for you to read? How did you feel while reading about some of the things Celie felt and experienced in her lifetime?

QUOTATIONS *The Color Purple*

1. "You better not never tell nobody but God."

2. "She ugly. He say. But she ain't no stranger to hard work. And she clean. And God done fixed her. You can do everything just like you want to and she ain't gonna make you feed it or clothe it."

3. "But I don't know how to fight. All I know how to do is stay alive."

4. "But I just say, Never mine, never mine, long as I can spell G-o-d I got somebody along."

5. "You ever hit her? Mr. _____ ast. Harpo look down at his hands. Naw suh, he say low, embarrass. Well how you spect to make her mind? Wives is like children. You have to let 'em know who got the upper hand. Nothing can do that better than a good sound beating."

6. "Mr. _____ marry me to take care of his children. I marry him cause my daddy made me. I don't love Mr. _____ and he don't love me."

7. "He don't want a wife, he want a dog."

8. "Most times I pretend I ain't there. He never know the difference. Never ast me how I feel, nothing. Just do his business, get off, go to sleep."

9. "Every time they ast me to do something, Miss Celie, I act like I'm you. I jump right up and do just what they say."

10. "They [white people] have the nerve to try to make us think slavery fell through because of us, say Sofia. Like us didn't have sense enough to handle it."

11. "If you was my wife, she say, I'd cover you up with kisses stead of licks, and work hard for you too."

12. "My mama die, I tell Shug. My sister Nettie run away. Mr. _____ come git me to take care his rotten children. He never ast me nothing bout myself. . . . Nobody ever love me, I say."

13. "All day long I act just like Sofia. I stutter. I mutter to myself. I stumble bout the house crazy for Mr. _____ blood. In my mind, he falling dead every which way."

14. "I remember one time you said your life made you feel so ashamed you couldn't even talk about it to God, you had to write it, bad as you thought your writing was."

15. "Oh, Celie, there are colored people in the world who want us to know! Want us to grow and see the light!"

16. "We are not white. We are not Europeans. We are black like the Africans themselves. And that we and the Africans will be working for a common goal: the uplift of black people everywhere."

17. "There is a way that the men speak to women that reminds me too much of Pa. They listen just long enough to issue instructions. They don't even look at women when women are speaking...The women also do not 'look in a man's face' as they say. To 'look in a man's face' is a brazen thing to do. They look instead at his feet or his knees. And what can I say to this? Again, it is our own behavior around Pa."

18. "I think Africans are very much like white people back home, in that they think they are the center of the universe and that everything that is done is done for them."

19. "He ain't notice me and probably wouldn't even if he looked at me."

20. "There is so much we don't understand. And so much unhappiness comes because of that."

21. "I think it pisses God off it you walk by the color purple in a field somewhere and don't notice it."

22. "Look at you. You black, you pore, you ugly, you a woman. Goddam, he say, you nothing at all."

23. "I'm pore, I'm black, I may be ugly and can't cook, a voice say to everything listening. But I'm here."

24. "Women weaker, he say. People think they weaker, say the weaker, anyhow. Women spose to take it easy. Cry if you want to. Not try to take over."

25. "Celie, I say, happiness was just a trick in your case."

26. "Everybody learn something in life, she say."

27. "I start to wonder why us need love. Why us suffer. Why us black. Why us men and women. Where do children really come from. It didn't take long to realize I didn't hardly know nothing. And that if you ast yourself why you black or a man or a woman or a bush it don't mean nothing if you don't ask why you here, period...I think us here to wonder, myself. To wonder. To ast. And that in wondering bout the big things and asting bout the big things, you learn about the little ones, almost by accident. But you never know nothing more about the big things than you start out with. The more I wonder, he say, the more I love."

28. "I feel a little peculiar round the children. For one thing, they grown. And I see they think me and Nettie and Shug and Albert and Samuel and Harpo and Sofia and Jack and Odessa real old and don't know much what going on. But I don't think us feel old at all. And us so happy. Matter of fact, I think this the youngest us ever felt."

LESSON SIXTEEN

Objectives
1. To discuss the novel on a deeper than direct-recall level
2. To prepare students for questions and topics covered on the test
3. To allow students to make personal connections with the text

Activity
Continue working on the Extra Discussion Questions as previously described.

LESSON SEVENTEEN

<u>Objectives</u>
1. To allow students to experience the story in a different medium
2. To get students to discuss the similarities and differences between the novel and the musical
3. To appreciate the qualities of both a novel and a musical

<u>Activity #1</u>
Purchase or download the music from the Broadway production of *The Color Purple*. Explain to students that the songs they are about to evaluate are from the musical production of the novel they just read. Before you begin the assignment, talk about the challenges involved in putting a novel into musical form. Next, put students into pairs and assign each pair a song from the musical. Provide students with the lyrics to their assigned songs (available at AllMusicals.com) and ask them to analyze the lyrics, comparing and contrasting what takes place in the song to what takes place in the novel. Once students have had sufficient time to evaluate their songs, come together as a class to listen to the songs and talk about the differences in the musical and the novel. Allow each group to present their information to the class and then play the song for others to hear. Afterward, hold a class discussion on whether or not the themes and emotions of the novel are conveyed in the musical version of the story. Ask students to reflect on how the musical version succeeded in sharing Celie's story and ask where there is room for improvement.

Note: Depending on class length and the number of students, you may wish to modify this activity. An alternative to looking at each song would be assigning only 4 or 5 songs to students and taking a closer look at the most influential songs in the musical. You can also use YouTube.com or idesktop.tv to allow your students to view excerpts of the musical online. Another alternative would be to show students the film version of *The Color Purple* and compare and contrast it with the novel.

LESSON EIGHTEEN

Objective
To review all of the vocabulary work done in this unit.

Activity
Choose one (or more) of the vocabulary review activities listed below and spend your class period as directed in the activity. Some of the materials for these review activities are located in the Vocabulary Resource Materials section in this LitPlan.

VOCABULARY REVIEW ACTIVITIES

1. Divide your class into two teams and have an old-fashioned spelling or definition bee.

2. Give each of your students (or students in groups of two, three or four) a *The Color Purple* Vocabulary Word Search Puzzle. The person (group) to find all of the vocabulary words in the puzzle first wins.

3. Give students a *The Color Purple* Vocabulary Word Search Puzzle without the word list. The person or group to find the most vocabulary words in the puzzle wins.

4. Use a *The Color Purple* Vocabulary Crossword Puzzle. Put the puzzle onto a transparency on the overhead projector (so everyone can see it), and do the puzzle together as a class.

5. Give students a *The Color Purple* Vocabulary Matching Worksheet to do.

6. Divide your class into two teams. Use *The Color Purple* vocabulary words with their letters jumbled as a word list. Student 1 from Team A faces off against Student 1 from Team B. You write the first jumbled word on the board. The first student (1A or 1B) to unscramble the word wins the chance for his/her team to score points. If 1A wins the jumble, go to student 2A and give him/her a definition. He/she must give you the correct spelling of the vocabulary word which fits that definition. If he/she does, Team A scores a point, and you give student 3A a definition for which you expect a correctly spelled matching vocabulary word. Continue giving Team A definitions until some team member makes an incorrect response. An incorrect response sends the game back to the jumbled-word face off, this time with students 2A and 2B. Instead of repeating giving definitions to the first few students of each team, continue with the student after the one who gave the last incorrect response on the team. For example, if Team B wins the jumbled-word face-off, and student 5B gave the last incorrect answer for Team B, you would start this round of definition questions with student 6B, and so on. The team with the most points wins!

7. Have students write a story in which they correctly use as many vocabulary words as possible. Have students read their compositions orally! Post the most original compositions on your bulletin board!

LESSON NINETEEN

Objective
　　To review the main ideas and events in *The Color Purple*

Activity
Choose one of the review games/activities suggested in this unit and spend your class time as directed there.

REVIEW GAMES/ACTIVITIES

1. Ask the class to make up a unit test for *The Color Purple*. The test should have 4 sections: matching, true/false, short answer, and essay. Students may use 1/2 period to make the test and then swap papers and use the other 1/2 class period to take a test a classmate has devised. (open book) You may want to use the unit test included in this packet or take questions from the students' unit tests to formulate your own test.

2. Take 1/2 period for students to make up true and false questions (including the answers). Collect the papers and divide the class into two teams. Draw a big tic-tac-toe board on the chalk board. Make one team X and one team O. Ask questions to each side, giving each student one turn. If the question is answered correctly, that students' team's letter (X or O) is placed in the box. If the answer is incorrect, no letter is placed in the box. The object is to get three in a row like tic-tac-toe. You may want to keep track of the number of games won for each team.

3. Take 1/2 period for students to make up questions (true/false and short answer). Collect the questions. Divide the class into two teams. You'll alternate asking questions to individual members of teams A & B (like in a spelling bee). The question keeps going from A to B until it is correctly answered, then a new question is asked. A correct answer does not allow the team to get another question. Correct answers are +2 points; incorrect answers are -1 point.

4. Have students pair up and quiz each other from their study guides and class notes.

5. Give students a *The Color Purple* crossword puzzle to complete.

6. Play What's My Line?. This is similar to the old television show. Students assume the roles of different characters from the novel. One student gives clues to the class, or to a panel of contestants. The contestants try to guess the identity of the guest. Students may enjoy assisting you in creating rules and procedures for the game.

7. Divide your class into two teams. Use *The Color Purple* crossword words with their letters jumbled as a word list. Student 1 from Team A faces off against Student 1 from Team B. You write the first jumbled word on the board. The first student (1A or 1B) to unscramble the word wins the chance for his/her team to score points. If 1A wins the jumble, go to student 2A and give him/her a clue. He/she must give you the correct word which matches that clue. If he/she does, Team A scores a point, and you give student 3A a clue for which you expect another correct response. Continue giving Team A clues until some team member makes an incorrect response. An incorrect response sends the game back to the jumbled-word face off, this time with students 2A and 2B. Instead of repeating giving clues to the first few students of each team, continue with the student after the one who gave the last incorrect response on the team. For example, if Team B wins the jumbled-word face-off, and student 5B gave the last incorrect answer for Team B, you would start this round of clue questions with student 6B, and so on. The team with the most points wins!

8. Play Jeopardy. Divide the class into two groups. Assign each group a category or book from the novel and have them devise answers for that category. Play the game according to the television show procedures.

9. Play Drawing in the Details. This is similar to Pictionary. Divide students into teams. A student from one team draws a scene from the novel. (You may want to specify the section.) Drawings should be kept simple, to keep the pace lively. Students in the opposing team locate the scene in their books and read it aloud. If they are incorrect, the illustrator's team has a chance to guess. Involve students in setting up a scoring system and any other necessary rules.

LESSON TWENTY

Objectives
To test the students understanding of the main ideas and themes in *The Color Purple*

Activity #1
Distribute the unit tests. Go over the instructions in detail and allow the students the entire class period to complete the exam.

NOTES ABOUT THE UNIT TESTS IN THIS UNIT:

There are 5 different unit tests included in the LitPlan Teacher Pack. Two are short answer, two are multiple choice. There is one advanced short answer test. The answers to the advanced short answer test will be based on the discussions you have had during class and should be graded accordingly. You should choose the tests and/or test parts which best suit your needs. Matching and short answer tests have answer keys. For essay type questions, grade according to your own criteria based on class discussions and the level of your students. Also, you will need to choose vocabulary words to read orally for the vocabulary section of the short answer tests.

Activity #2
Collect all test papers and assigned books prior to the end of the class period.

UNIT TESTS

The Color Purple Short Answer Unit Test 1

I. Matching

____ 1. FATHER A. He reveals the true story about Nettie and Celie's father.
____ 2. DIAPER B. Tashi's boyfriend
____ 3. LETTERS C. She fights back when her husband beats her.
____ 4. SONG D. Mother of Olivia and Adam
____ 5. PANTS E. Sofia fights with Harpo about being this.
____ 6. ROOFLEAF F. Sofia's husband
____ 7. SISTER G. Celie's was lynched for running a successful business
____ 8. QUILT H. Mr. ___ hides her letters from Celie.
____ 9. PALLBEARER I. The only piece of mail Albert ever gives Celie directly
____ 10. TELEGRAM J. Albert & Celie both love her.
____ 11. SQUEAK K. What Corrine would like Nettie to call her
____ 12. SHUG L. How Celie knows what is going on in Nettie's life
____ 13. SOFIA M. The Olinka worship it.
____ 14. HARPO N. Shug writes & sings this for Celie
____ 15. ALBERT O. Nettie uses this to remind Corrine she had once met the mother of Adam and Olivia.
____ 16. CELIE P. "Olivia" is embroidered on this.
____ 17. NETTIE Q. Celie starts a business making these.
____ 18. SAMUEL R. Mr. ___
____ 19. ADAM S. Shug is in love with this 19 year-old musician.
____ 20. GERMAINE T. Mary Agnes

II. Short Answer

1. How many times has Celie given birth? Who is the father?

2. What does Celie discover about her daughter? How does she make this discovery?

3. Who is Shug Avery?

4. Why is Celie jealous of Sofia?

5. How many children do Shug and Albert have together? Where are their children?

6. Celie tells Shug that Mr. ___ will beat her when she is gone. When Shug asks why, what is Celie's response?

7. Why is Sofia in jail?

8. What is the plan for getting Sofia out of jail?

9. How do Celie and Shug get the rest of Nettie's letters without Albert's realizing they have them?

10. What does Celie discover about the two children she had with her father?

11. What surprises Nettie about slavery?

12. Who does Corrine believe are Adam and Olivia's birth parents?

13. Why are the Olinka happy to see there is a road being built to their village? What later upsets them about the road?

14. Why had Samuel urged Nettie to come to Africa?

15. Why doesn't Celie write to God anymore?

16. After moving to Memphis, what type of business does Celie start? What is the name of the business?

17. What does Celie learn about Mr. _____ and how he's been living since she moved away?

18. What happens to Nettie and Samuel's relationship when they travel to England?

19. What does Albert ask Celie? What is her response?

20. With whom is Celie reunited with at the end of the novel?

III. Composition
1. What does Celie learn over the course of the novel? How does she grow and change as a result of events that take place in her life? Support your answer with details from the text.

IV. Vocabulary

Write the vocabulary words you are given. After writing them down, go back and write in their definitions.

Word	Definition
1	
2	
3	
4	
5	
6	
7	
8	
9	
10	

The Color Purple Short Answer Unit Test 1 Answer Key

I. Matching

G	1.	FATHER	A.	He reveals the true story about Nettie and Celie's father.
P	2.	DIAPER	B.	Tashi's boyfriend
L	3.	LETTERS	C.	She fights back when her husband beats her.
N	4.	SONG	D.	Mother of Olivia and Adam
Q	5.	PANTS	E.	Sofia fights with Harpo about being this.
M	6.	ROOFLEAF	F.	Sofia's husband
K	7.	SISTER	G.	Celie's was lynched for running a successful business
O	8.	QUILT	H.	Mr. ___ hides her letters from Celie.
E	9.	PALLBEARER	I.	The only piece of mail Albert ever gives Celie directly
I	10.	TELEGRAM	J.	Albert & Celie both love her.
T	11.	SQUEAK	K.	What Corrine would like Nettie to call her
J	12.	SHUG	L.	How Celie knows what is going on in Nettie's life
C	13.	SOFIA	M.	The Olinka worship it.
F	14.	HARPO	N.	Shug writes & sings this for Celie
R	15.	ALBERT	O.	Nettie uses this to remind Corrine she had once met the mother of Adam and Olivia.
D	16.	CELIE	P.	"Olivia" is embroidered on this.
H	17.	NETTIE	Q.	Celie starts a business making these.
A	18.	SAMUEL	R.	Mr. ___
B	19.	ADAM	S.	Shug is in love with this 19 year-old musician.
S	20.	GERMAINE	T.	Mary Agnes

II. Short Answer
1. How many times has Celie given birth? Who is the father?
   Celie has given birth twice, and Celie's father is the father of both children.
2. What does Celie discover about her daughter? How does she make this discovery?
   Celie discovers that her daughter is still alive. While in town, Celie sees a little girl that looks just like Celie and her daddy. When Celie asks the child's name, the little girl's mother tells Celie that the child's name is Pauline, but she calls her Olivia. Olivia is the name Celie had embroidered on her daughter's diapers.
3. Who is Shug Avery?
   She is a singer who performs in the area. Mr. ___'s sisters allude to a romantic relationship between Mr. ___ and Shug.
4. Why is Celie jealous of Sofia?
   Celie tells Sofia that she is jealous of her strength and will to fight back.
5. How many children do Shug and Albert have together? Where are their children?
   They have three children who are living with Shug's mother.
6. Celie tells Shug that Mr. ___ will beat her when she is gone. When Shug asks why, what is Celie's response?
   Celie says it is because she is Celie, not Shug.
7. Why is Sofia in jail?
   Sofia was in town with her kids when the mayor's wife, a white woman, saw how clean and well-kept Sofia's kids were. When she asked Sofia if she would like to be her maid, Sofia said, "Hell no." The mayor was offended and slapped Sofia. Sofia punched the mayor. Police then came, beat Sofia severely, and threw her in jail.
8. What is the plan for getting Sofia out of jail?
   The plan is to tell the warden that Sofia is happy in jail since she does less work there than at home. Squeak plans to tell the warden that the way to really punish her is to make her work for a white woman. This way Sofia can have a better life, and the warden can feel like he is making her suffer.
9. How do Celie and Shug get the rest of Nettie's letters without Albert's realizing they have them?
   Shug gets the keys to Albert's trunk where all the letters are hidden. They steam open the envelopes and take out the letters, putting the empty envelopes back in the trunk.
10. What does Celie discover about the two children she had with her father?
    They are both growing up in a house full of love. Samuel and Corrine adopted them but have no idea that Nettie, the person helping to care for their children, is their aunt and sister.
11. What surprises Nettie about slavery?
    That Africans used to capture their own people and sell them into the slave trade surprises Nettie.
12. Who does Corrine believe are Adam and Olivia's birth parents?
    Corrine believes Nettie and Samuel are Adam and Olivia's birth parents. She does not know they are actually Celie's children by Celie's own father.
13. Why are the Olinka happy to see there is a road being built to their village? What later upsets them about the road?
    At first the Olinka are happy to see there is a road being built to their village since it will make travel much quicker and easier to and from the village. However, they are later upset to learn that the road is not stopping at their village but going straight through it and destroying several buildings, including the school and church. The road builders have guns and use force to ensure they road is built despite the fact the Olinka people own the land.

14. Why had Samuel urged Nettie to come to Africa?
    Samuel had urged Nettie to come to Africa because he thought Adam and Olivia were Nettie's children, and he wanted her to be with them.

15. Why doesn't Celie write to God anymore?
    Celie doesn't write to God anymore because she thinks God is a man. All the men in her life have always been no-good and let her down, just as she feels God has.

16. After moving to Memphis, what type of business does Celie start? What is the name of the business?
    Celie begins her own pants business. She calls it "Folkspants, Unlimited."

17. What does Celie learn about Mr. _____ and how he's been living since she moved away?
    Celie learns Mr. _____ has been working very hard in the fields and keeping the house up nicely.

18. What happens to Nettie and Samuel's relationship when they travel to England?
    They realize their love for each other and get married.

19. What does Albert ask Celie? What is her response?
    Albert asks Celie to marry him again, but this time in spirit and flesh. She refuses and asks if they can just be friends.

20. With whom is Celie reunited with at the end of the novel?
    Much to Celie's surprise and delight, Nettie returns, and she is reunited with Nettie, Adam, and Olivia.

IV. Vocabulary
    Write the vocabulary words and definitions you will use for this test.

Word	Definition
1	
2	
3	
4	
5	
6	
7	
8	
9	
10	

The Color Purple Short Answer Unit Test 2

I. Matching

    ____ 1. FATHER   A. Mary Agnes

    ____ 2. DIAPER   B. Mr. ___ hides her letters from Celie.

    ____ 3. LETTERS   C. He reveals the true story about Nettie and Celie's father.

    ____ 4. SONG   D. Sofia's husband

    ____ 5. PANTS   E. Mr. ___

    ____ 6. ROOFLEAF   F. The only piece of mail Albert ever gives Celie directly

    ____ 7. SISTER   G. She fights back when her husband beats her.

    ____ 8. QUILT   H. Nettie uses this to remind Corrine she had once met the mother of Adam and Olivia.

    ____ 9. PALLBEARER   I. Shug writes & sings this for Celie

    ____ 10. TELEGRAM   J. Mother of Olivia and Adam

    ____ 11. SQUEAK   K. Celie starts a business making these.

    ____ 12. SHUG   L. Tashi's boyfriend

    ____ 13. SOFIA   M. The Olinka worship it.

    ____ 14. HARPO   N. Sofia fights with Harpo about being this.

    ____ 15. ALBERT   O. Shug is in love with this 19 year-old musician.

    ____ 16. CELIE   P. "Olivia" is embroidered on this.

    ____ 17. NETTIE   Q. Celie's was lynched for running a successful business

    ____ 18. SAMUEL   R. How Celie knows what is going on in Nettie's life

    ____ 19. ADAM   S. Albert & Celie both love her.

    ____ 20. GERMAINE   T. What Corrine would like Nettie to call her

II. Short Answer

1. How many times has Celie given birth? Who is the father?

2. What kind of a business does Harpo start, and where does he open it?

3. Who is Squeak, and how did she lose two of her teeth?

4. Why is Sofia in jail?

5. How do Celie and Shug get the rest of Nettie's letters without Albert's realizing they have them?

6. What does Celie discover about the two children she had with her father?

7. What does Shug teach Celie about God?

8. How are the Olinka people treated after the rubber factory is built?

9. What reasons does Tashi give for refusing to marry Adam?

10. What does Adam do to prove his love and devotion to Tashi?

III. Quotations: Explain the importance and meaning of the following quotations:

1. "Every time they ast me to do something, Miss Celie, I act like I'm you. I jump right up and do just what they say."

2. "I remember one time you said your life made you feel so ashamed you couldn't even talk about it to God, you had to write it, bad as you thought your writing was."

3. "I'm pore, I'm black, I may be ugly and can't cook, a voice say to everything listening. But I'm here."

4. "I start to wonder why us need love. Why us suffer. Why us black. Why us men and women. Where do children really come from. It didn't take long to realize I didn't hardly know nothing. And that if you ast yourself why you black or a man or a woman or a bush it don't mean nothing if you don't ask why you here, period...I think us here to wonder, myself. To wonder. To ast. And that in wondering bout the big things and asting bout the big things, you learn about the little ones, almost by accident. But you never know nothing more about the big things than you start out with. The more I wonder, he say, the more I love."

IV. Composition
1. How does Celie's view of God change over the course of the novel?

2. What is the significance of the title of the novel?

V. Vocabulary
   Write the vocabulary words you are given. After writing them down, go back and write in their definitions.

Word	Definition
1	
2	
3	
4	
5	
6	
7	
8	
9	
10	

The Color Purple Short Answer Unit Test 2 Answer Key

I. Matching

Q	1.	FATHER	A.	Mary Agnes
P	2.	DIAPER	B.	Mr. ___ hides her letters from Celie.
R	3.	LETTERS	C.	He reveals the true story about Nettie and Celie's father.
I	4.	SONG	D.	Sofia's husband
K	5.	PANTS	E.	Mr. ___
M	6.	ROOFLEAF	F.	The only piece of mail Albert ever gives Celie directly
T	7.	SISTER	G.	She fights back when her husband beats her.
H	8.	QUILT	H.	Nettie uses this to remind Corrine she had once met the mother of Adam and Olivia.
N	9.	PALLBEARER	I.	Shug writes & sings this for Celie
F	10.	TELEGRAM	J.	Mother of Olivia and Adam
A	11.	SQUEAK	K.	Celie starts a business making these.
S	12.	SHUG	L.	Tashi's boyfriend
G	13.	SOFIA	M.	The Olinka worship it.
D	14.	HARPO	N.	Sofia fights with Harpo about being this.
E	15.	ALBERT	O.	Shug is in love with this 19 year-old musician.
J	16.	CELIE	P.	"Olivia" is embroidered on this.
B	17.	NETTIE	Q.	Celie's was lynched for running a successful business
C	18.	SAMUEL	R.	How Celie knows what is going on in Nettie's life
L	19.	ADAM	S.	Albert & Celie both love her.
O	20.	GERMAINE	T.	What Corrine would like Nettie to call her

II. Short Answer
1. How many times has Celie given birth? Who is the father?
   Celie has given birth twice, and Celie's father is the father of both children.

2. What kind of a business does Harpo start, and where does he open it?
   Harpo opens a jukejoint in his and Sofia's home.

3. Who is Squeak, and how did she lose two of her teeth?
   Squeak is Harpo's girlfriend. She called Sofia a bitch and told her to stop dancing with her man. She then slapped Sofia, and Sofia punched her back, knocking out two of her teeth.

4. Why is Sofia in jail?
   Sofia was in town with her kids when the mayor's wife, a white woman, saw how clean and well-kept Sofia's kids were. When she asked Sofia if she would like to be her maid, Sofia said, "Hell no." The mayor was offended and slapped Sofia. Sofia punched the mayor. Police then came, beat Sofia severely, and threw her in jail.

5. How do Celie and Shug get the rest of Nettie's letters without Albert's realizing they have them?
   Shug gets the keys to Albert's trunk where all the letters are hidden. They steam open the envelopes and take out the letters, putting the empty envelopes back in the trunk.

6. What does Celie discover about the two children she had with her father?
   They are both growing up in a house full of love. Samuel and Corrine adopted them but have no idea that Nettie, the person helping to care for their children, is their aunt and sister.

7. What does Shug teach Celie about God?
   Shug tells Celie that God isn't a man or a woman, but an It. She tells Celie to get the image of God being an old white man out of her head and to start seeing God in the world that is all around her. She tells her God is inside everyone, and they just have to find it. She says that God loves all people and just wants to be loved and appreciated back.

8. How are the Olinka people treated after the rubber factory is built?
   They are forced to move to a barren area of land that is without water six months of the year. In this time, they must pay the factory for water. There is also no more roofleaf left, leaving the Olinka people without their item of worship.

9. What reasons does Tashi give for refusing to marry Adam?
   She is worried Americans will look down on her because of the scarification marks on her face and because of her very dark skin. She is also worried Adam will find someone else to love in America, and she will then be all alone in a strange country with no family.

10. What does Adam do to prove his love and devotion to Tashi?
    Adam has his face scarred to look like Tashi's.

V. Vocabulary
    Write the vocabulary words and definitions you will use for this test.

Word	Definition
1	
2	
3	
4	
5	
6	
7	
8	
9	
10	

The Color Purple Advanced Short Answer Unit Test

I. Matching

____ 1.	FATHER	A.	She fights back when her husband beats her.
____ 2.	DIAPER	B.	Albert & Celie both love her.
____ 3.	LETTERS	C.	The Olinka worship it.
____ 4.	SONG	D.	Shug is in love with this 19 year-old musician.
____ 5.	PANTS	E.	Tashi's boyfriend
____ 6.	ROOFLEAF	F.	Mary Agnes
____ 7.	SISTER	G.	Sofia's husband
____ 8.	QUILT	H.	Celie's was lynched for running a successful business
____ 9.	PALLBEARER	I.	Mother of Olivia and Adam
____ 10.	TELEGRAM	J.	Shug writes & sings this for Celie
____ 11.	SQUEAK	K.	Mr. ___
____ 12.	SHUG	L.	He reveals the true story about Nettie and Celie's father.
____ 13.	SOFIA	M.	The only piece of mail Albert ever gives Celie directly
____ 14.	HARPO	N.	What Corrine would like Nettie to call her
____ 15.	ALBERT	O.	Sofia fights with Harpo about being this.
____ 16.	CELIE	P.	How Celie knows what is going on in Nettie's life
____ 17.	NETTIE	Q.	Nettie uses this to remind Corrine she had once met the mother of Adam and Olivia.
____ 18.	SAMUEL	R.	"Olivia" is embroidered on this.
____ 19.	ADAM	S.	Mr. ___ hides her letters from Celie.
____ 20.	GERMAINE	T.	Celie starts a business making these.

II. Short Answer
1. How does Celie feel about standing up for herself and fighting back against others who don't treat her properly? How does this change over the course of the novel? Use evidence from the text to support your answer.

2. How does Nettie's perception of colored people and white people change as she leaves her home town and heads out into the world?

3. The characters in the novel have a lot to be angry about. Several characters treat each other inappropriately and without respect. However, they are usually able to forgive each other quickly, understanding the hardships they too are enduring. What does this say about the characters in the novel? What does this say about the life of black people in this time? Use specific examples from the novel to support your answer.

4. Compare and contrast the story Samuel was told about Adam and Olivia with the truth that Nettie knows. What surprises do both Nettie and Samuel receive?

5. How does Celie's view of God change over the course of the novel?

6. Compare and contrast what Albert means when he says, "Look at you. You black, you pore, you ugly, you a woman. Goddam, he say, you nothing at all," with what Celie means when she says, "I'm pore, I'm black, I may be ugly and can't cook, a voice say to everything listening. But I'm here."

7. Why does Tashi decide to scar her face and go through with female circumcision? How do her views on these tribal traditions vary from the views of Adam and Olivia?

8. What is the significance of the title of the novel?

9. What does Celie learn over the course of the novel? How does she grow and change as a result of events that take place in her life? Support your answer with details from the text.

10. Describe the relationship between Celie and Shug. How does in grow and change over the course of the novel? What does each character give and take from that relationship? How does it help both Celie and Shug?

III. Quotations: Explain the importance and meaning of the following quotations:

1. "Every time they ast me to do something, Miss Celie, I act like I'm you. I jump right up and do just what they say."

2. "They [white people] have the nerve to try to make us think slavery fell through because of us, say Sofia. Like us didn't have sense enough to handle it."

3. "If you was my wife, she say, I'd cover you up with kisses stead of licks, and work hard for you too."

4. "My mama die, I tell Shug. My sister Nettie run away. Mr. _____ come git me to take care his rotten children. He never ast me nothing bout myself. He clam on top of me and fuck and fuck, even when my head bandaged. Nobody ever love me, I say."

5. "I remember one time you said your life made you feel so ashamed you couldn't even talk about it to God, you had to write it, bad as you thought your writing was."

6. "There is a way that the men speak to women that reminds me too much of Pa. They listen just long enough to issue instructions. They don't even look at women when women are speaking...The women also do not 'look in a man's face' as they say. To 'look in a man's face' is a brazen thing to do. They look instead at his feet or his knees. And what can I say to this? Again, it is our own behavior around Pa."

7. "There is so much we don't understand. And so much unhappiness comes because of that."

8. "I start to wonder why us need love. Why us suffer. Why us black. Why us men and women. Where do children really come from. It didn't take long to realize I didn't hardly know nothing. And that if you ast yourself why you black or a man or a woman or a bush it don't mean nothing if you don't ask why you here, period...I think us here to wonder, myself. To wonder. To ast. And that in wondering bout the big things and asting bout the big things, you learn about the little ones, almost by accident. But you never know nothing more about the big things than you start out with. The more I wonder, he say, the more I love."

IV. Composition
1. What is the author trying to say about gender roles throughout the novel? Use examples from the text to support your answer.

2. Sofia put it best when she said, "Everybody learn something in life." Several characters change over the course of the novel, learning from the events that take place in their lives. Select three characters from the novel and outline how they change as a result of events in the story.

V. Vocabulary

    A. Write the vocabulary words you are given. After writing them down, go back and write in their definitions.

Word	Definition
1	
2	
3	
4	
5	
6	
7	
8	
9	
10	

    B. Write a paragraph about the book using 8 of the 10 vocabulary words above.

The Color Purple Advanced Short Answer Unit Test Answer Key

I. Matching

H	1.	FATHER	A.	She fights back when her husband beats her.
R	2.	DIAPER	B.	Albert & Celie both love her.
P	3.	LETTERS	C.	The Olinka worship it.
J	4.	SONG	D.	Shug is in love with this 19 year-old musician.
T	5.	PANTS	E.	Tashi's boyfriend
C	6.	ROOFLEAF	F.	Mary Agnes
N	7.	SISTER	G.	Sofia's husband
Q	8.	QUILT	H.	Celie's was lynched for running a successful business
O	9.	PALLBEARER	I.	Mother of Olivia and Adam
M	10.	TELEGRAM	J.	Shug writes & sings this for Celie
F	11.	SQUEAK	K.	Mr. ___
B	12.	SHUG	L.	He reveals the true story about Nettie and Celie's father.
A	13.	SOFIA	M.	The only piece of mail Albert ever gives Celie directly
G	14.	HARPO	N.	What Corrine would like Nettie to call her
K	15.	ALBERT	O.	Sofia fights with Harpo about being this.
I	16.	CELIE	P.	How Celie knows what is going on in Nettie's life
S	17.	NETTIE	Q.	Nettie uses this to remind Corrine she had once met the mother of Adam and Olivia.
L	18.	SAMUEL	R.	"Olivia" is embroidered on this.
E	19.	ADAM	S.	Mr. ___ hides her letters from Celie.
D	20.	GERMAINE	T.	Celie starts a business making these.

V. Vocabulary
   Write the vocabulary words and definitions you will use for this test.

Word	Definition
1	
2	
3	
4	
5	
6	
7	
8	
9	
10	

The Color Purple Multiple Choice Unit Test 1

I. Matching

____ 1.	FATHER	A.	He reveals the true story about Nettie and Celie's father.
____ 2.	DIAPER	B.	Sofia fights with Harpo about being this.
____ 3.	LETTERS	C.	Mr. ___ hides her letters from Celie.
____ 4.	SONG	D.	Shug is in love with this 19 year-old musician.
____ 5.	PANTS	E.	Sofia's husband
____ 6.	ROOFLEAF	F.	She fights back when her husband beats her.
____ 7.	SISTER	G.	What Corrine would like Nettie to call her
____ 8.	QUILT	H.	Albert & Celie both love her.
____ 9.	PALLBEARER	I.	Nettie uses this to remind Corrine she had once met the mother of Adam and Olivia.
____ 10.	TELEGRAM	J.	Celie's was lynched for running a successful business
____ 11.	SQUEAK	K.	Mr. ___
____ 12.	SHUG	L.	Tashi's boyfriend
____ 13.	SOFIA	M.	The Olinka worship it.
____ 14.	HARPO	N.	Celie starts a business making these.
____ 15.	ALBERT	O.	"Olivia" is embroidered on this.
____ 16.	CELIE	P.	Shug writes & sings this for Celie
____ 17.	NETTIE	Q.	Mary Agnes
____ 18.	SAMUEL	R.	How Celie knows what is going on in Nettie's life
____ 19.	ADAM	S.	Mother of Olivia and Adam
____ 20.	GERMAINE	T.	The only piece of mail Albert ever gives Celie directly

II. Multiple Choice

1. Who is Shug Avery?
    A. She is Mr. _____'s sister who comes to stay with them for a while. Her husband beat her and she ran away to the safety of her older brother.
    B. She is a singer who travels the area performing. Mr. _____'s sisters allude to a romantic relationship between Mr. _____ and Shug.
    C. She is the wife of the Reverend. She helps Celie adjust to her new life as the wife of a selfish man and the mother of four children who hate her.
    D. She is a school teacher who secretly continues to tutor Celie even though she is already married. She knows Celie is smart and helps her to keep learning to one day get away from Mr. _____.

2. How many times has Celie given birth? Who is the father?
    A. She has three children by three different fathers.
    B. She has four children by the white man for whom her father works.
    C. She has one child by the school teacher.
    D. She has two children by her father.

3. Why is Celie jealous of Sofia?
    A. Celie is jealous of Sofia's natural beauty.
    B. Celie tells Sofia that she is jealous of her relationsip with Harpo.
    C. Celie is jealous because Sofia was able to keep all her children.
    D. Celie tells Sofia that she is jealous of her ability to fight back.

4. What does Celie discover about her daughter?
    A. Celie discovers her daughter is buried in the local cemetery.
    B. Celie discovers her daughter is being raised by a man and his wife who run the general store in Monticello.
    C. Celie discovers her daughter is in a orphanage in Georgia.
    D. Celie discovers her daughter is still alive.

5. How many children do Shug and Albert have together? Where are their children?
    A. They have two children who live with Shug's youngest sister.
    B. They have three children who live with Shug's mother.
    C. They have five children, but three died. They live with Albert's sister.
    D. They have four children who live with two different adoptive families.

6. Celie tells Shug that Mr. ___ will beat her when she is gone. When Shug asks why, what is Celie's response?
    A. Celie says it is because she is Celie, not Nettie.
    B. Celie says it is because she is Celie, not Shug.
    C. Celie says it is because Mr. ___ hates her.
    D. Celie says it is because Mr. ___ is nicer when Shug is around.

7. Why is Sofia in jail?
    A. The mayor's wife asked Sofia if she would like to be her maid and Sofia said, "Hell no." The mayor was offended and slapped Sofia. She punched the mayor and was thrown in jail.
    B. The store owner tries to cheat Sofia when she is buying cloth. She argues with him. He throws her out, keeping her money and not giving her any cloth. She bangs on the locked door and yells and is arrested for disrupting the peace.
    C. Sofia attacks Squeak when she sees her hugging Harpo. Harpo pulls Sofia off his girlfriend, and Sofia's date slugs Harpo for touching Sofia. The place gets so rowdy, the police arrive and Sofia is arrested with a number of others.
    D. Sofia is in town and begins to feel sick. She cannot find a Colored bathroom, so she sneaks into the white bathroom. On her way out, she gets caught by a shop owner who immediately calls the police.

8. What is the plan for getting Sofia out of jail?
    A. To try to make the case that Sofia is mentally unstable, getting her to a mental hospital or back home in the care of her family
    B. To tell the warden Sofia is happy in jail and the way to really punish her is to make her work for a white woman
    C. To get dynamite from the people building a nearby bridge and bust her out one night
    D. To ask for parole for good behavior, pleading for Sofia to be back with her six children and under house arrest

9. How do Celie and Shug get the rest of Nettie's letters without Albert's realizing they have them?
    A. Celie and Albert go to church while Shug goes through Albert's trunk to find the letters, later hiding them under Celie's pillow for her to read that night.
    B. Shug confronts Albert about the letter and refuses to speak to him ever again if he doesn't come clean with Celie and let her have her letters.
    C. Shug leaves the key for Celie while she takes Albert to the jukejoint for the night to get drunk, thinking Celie should have enough time to read most of the letters.
    D. Shug gets the keys to Albert's trunk. They steam open the envelopes, taking out the letters and putting the empty envelopes back in the trunk.

10. What does Celie discover about the two children she had with her father?
    A. Celie discovers her children are living with their father's aunt.
    B. Celie discovers her children are living in an orphanage outside of town.
    C. Celie discovers her children are dead.
    D. Celie discovers her children are alive and have been adopted by Samuel and Corrine.

11. What surprises Nettie about slavery?
    A. America wasn't the only country that had slaves.
    B. Slaves used to be severely beaten and many died from cruel treatment.
    C. That Africans used to capture their own people and sell them into the slave trade.
    D. People used to be auctioned off like cattle at town markets.

12. Why are the Olinka happy to see there is a road being built to their village? What later upsets them about the road?
    A. They are happy since it will allow for increased trade with neighboring villages, making survival in the rainy season much easier. They are later upset to learn they will have to pay a large fee to use the road, making trade nearly impossible.
    B. They are happy since it will make travel much quicker and easier to and from the village. They are later upset to learn the road is not stopping at their village but going straight through it and destroying several buildings.
    C. They are happy since it will finally allow for their village to have modern amenities like those found in larger cities. They are later upset to learn that the road is not sturdy enough to survive the rainy season and will be destroyed after only a few months of use.
    D. They are happy since it is providing work for many people of their village in a time when money is tight. They are later upset because the men do not pay them as promised, and the Olinka realize they worked hard for nothing in return.

13. Who does Corrine believe are Adam and Olivia's parents?
    A. Corrine believes Nettie and Mr. ____ are Adam and Olivia's birth parents.
    B. Corrine believes Nettie and Samuel are Adam and Olivia's birth parents.
    C. Corrine believes Celie and Albert are Adam and Olivia's birth parents.
    D. Corrine believes Celie and Samuel are Adam and Olivia's birth parents.

14. Why had Samuel urged Nettie to come to Africa?
    A. Samuel urged Nettie to come to Africa because he saw how close she and Olivia were and thought it would make the journey easier for Olivia.
    B. Samuel urged Nettie to come to Africa because he thought Adam and Olivia were Nettie's children, and he wanted them to be together.
    C. Samuel urged Nettie to come to Africa because he had fallen in love with her.
    D. Samuel urged Nettie to come to Africa because he knew Corrine would never be able to take care of the children.

15. Why doesn't Celie write to God anymore?
    A. Celie doesn't write to God anymore because she is writing to Shug.
    B. Celie doesn't write to God anymore because she thinks God is a man and all the men in her life are no-good and always let her down.
    C. Celie doesn't write to God anymore because she can now write to Nettie.
    D. Celie doesn't write to God anymore because she feels she is storng enough to handle her problems herself.

16. After moving to Memphis, what type of business does Celie start? What is the name of the business?
    A. Celie begins her own laundry business and she calls it "Cleanclothes, Unlimited."
    B. Celie begins her own pants business and she calls it "Pantsfolks, Unlimited."
    C. Celie begins her own laundry business and she calls it "Cleanfolks, Unlimited."
    D. Celie begins her own pants business and she calls it "Folkspants, Unlimited."

17. What does Celie learn about Mr. _____ and how he's been living since she moved away?
    A. Mr. _____ hired help for the fields and got a job in town working for the county jail. He makes enough money to live from his job and is creating a savings account with the money made off his land.
    B. Mr. _____ has been working very hard in the fields and keeping the house up nicely.
    C. Mr. _____ hired a young woman to live with him to help around the house and keep up with the cooking.
    D. Mr. _____'s older sister moved in with her three children after her husband was killed. Mr. _____ has been supporting the family for a few months now.

18. What happens to Nettie and Samuel's relationship when they travel to England?
    A. They grow closer in their friendship and decide to always stay in touch no matter what happens.
    B. They argue about whether or not to send the children to school in England or take them back to Africa and damage their friendship.
    C. They realize it is too hard to be friends without Corrine around and decide to go their separate ways.
    D. They realize their love for each other and get married.

19. What does Albert ask Celie? What is her response?
    A. He asks her to help him win back Shug. She says she loves Shug too and is trying to win her back herself.
    B. He asks her to marry him again, but this time in spirit and flesh. She says no and asks if they can just be friends.
    C. He asks her if she hates him for all the times he mistreated her over the years. She says she has finally forgiven him.
    D. He asks her if he can make shirts to go with her pants to sell them as sets. She says he can make shirts, but she won't sell them as part of her business.

20. Who is Celie reunited with at the end of the novel?
    A. Nettie, Olivia, and Adam
    B. Her mother
    C. Shug and her two children
    D. Her old school teacher

III. Composition
1. The characters in the novel have a lot to be angry about. Several characters treat each other inappropriately and without respect. However, they are usually able to forgive each other quickly, understanding the hardships they too are enduring. What does this say about the characters in the novel? What does this say about the life of black people in this time? Use specific examples from the novel to support your answer.

2. What does Celie learn over the course of the novel? How does she grow and change as a result of events that take place in her life? Support your answer with details from the text.

IV. Vocabulary

____ 1. HOSPITALITY	A. Tiresome by reason of length, slowness, or dullness

____ 2. FRACTIOUS	B. Strong distaste or objection

____ 3. VOUCH	C. The act of banishing or excluding

____ 4. AFFLICTION	D. Attitude of not caring one way or another

____ 5. DIGNITY	E. Quality of being worthy of respect

____ 6. SERENE	F. Defiant; shameless

____ 7. CONSCIENTIOUS	G. Inborn; existing from birth

____ 8. BRAZEN	H. Meticulously careful; dutiful

____ 9. APTITUDE	I. Guarantee; certify; attest to

____ 10. OSTRACISM	J. Taking another's possessions or rights gradually or stealthily

____ 11. INNATE	K. Engrossed; had one's attention held

____ 12. TEDIOUS	L. A condition of pain, suffering, or distress

____ 13. PIOUS	M. Having or exhibiting religious reverence; devout

____ 14. RECLUSE	N. Inclined to make trouble

____ 15. ENCROACHMENTS	O. Capability; ability

____ 16. RIVETED	P. Calm, peaceful, or tranquil

____ 17. SOJOURN	Q. A temporary stay

____ 18. NAIVE	R. The treatment of guests and strangers in a warm, friendly, generous way

____ 19. INDIFFERENCE	S. Lacking worldly experience and understanding; lacking sophistication

____ 20. REPUGNANCE	T. A person who lives in seclusion or apart from society

The Color Purple Multiple Choice Unit Test 1 Answer Key

I. Matching

J	1.	FATHER	A.	He reveals the true story about Nettie and Celie's father.
O	2.	DIAPER	B.	Sofia fights with Harpo about being this.
R	3.	LETTERS	C.	Mr. ___ hides her letters from Celie.
P	4.	SONG	D.	Shug is in love with this 19 year-old musician.
N	5.	PANTS	E.	Sofia's husband
M	6.	ROOFLEAF	F.	She fights back when her husband beats her.
G	7.	SISTER	G.	What Corrine would like Nettie to call her
I	8.	QUILT	H.	Albert & Celie both love her.
B	9.	PALLBEARER	I.	Nettie uses this to remind Corrine she had once met the mother of Adam and Olivia.
T	10.	TELEGRAM	J.	Celie's was lynched for running a successful business
Q	11.	SQUEAK	K.	Mr. ___
H	12.	SHUG	L.	Tashi's boyfriend
F	13.	SOFIA	M.	The Olinka worship it.
E	14.	HARPO	N.	Celie starts a business making these.
K	15.	ALBERT	O.	"Olivia" is embroidered on this.
S	16.	CELIE	P.	Shug writes & sings this for Celie
C	17.	NETTIE	Q.	Mary Agnes
A	18.	SAMUEL	R.	How Celie knows what is going on in Nettie's life
L	19.	ADAM	S.	Mother of Olivia and Adam
D	20.	GERMAINE	T.	The only piece of mail Albert ever gives Celie directly

II. Multiple Choice

B 1. Who is Shug Avery?
  A. She is Mr. _____'s sister who comes to stay with them for a while. Her husband beat her and she ran away to the safety of her older brother.
  B. She is a singer who travels the area performing. Mr. _____'s sisters allude to a romantic relationship between Mr. _____ and Shug.
  C. She is the wife of the Reverend. She helps Celie adjust to her new life as the wife of a selfish man and the mother of four children who hate her.
  D. She is a school teacher who secretly continues to tutor Celie even though she is already married. She knows Celie is smart and helps her to keep learning to one day get away from Mr. _____.

D 2. How many times has Celie given birth? Who is the father?
  A. She has three children by three different fathers.
  B. She has four children by the white man for whom her father works.
  C. She has one child by the school teacher.
  D. She has two children by her father.

D 3. Why is Celie jealous of Sofia?
  A. Celie is jealous of Sofia's natural beauty.
  B. Celie tells Sofia that she is jealous of her relationsip with Harpo.
  C. Celie is jealous because Sofia was able to keep all her children.
  D. Celie tells Sofia that she is jealous of her ability to fight back.

D 4. What does Celie discover about her daughter?
  A. Celie discovers her daughter is buried in the local cemetery.
  B. Celie discovers her daughter is being raised by a man and his wife who run the general store in Monticello.
  C. Celie discovers her daughter is in a orphanage in Georgia.
  D. Celie discovers her daughter is still alive.

B 5. How many children do Shug and Albert have together? Where are their children?
  A. They have two children who live with Shug's youngest sister.
  B. They have three children who live with Shug's mother.
  C. They have five children, but three died. They live with Albert's sister.
  D. They have four children who live with two different adoptive families.

B 6. Celie tells Shug that Mr. ___ will beat her when she is gone. When Shug asks why, what is Celie's response?
- A. Celie says it is because she is Celie, not Nettie.
- B. Celie says it is because she is Celie, not Shug.
- C. Celie says it is because Mr. ___ hates her.
- D. Celie says it is because Mr. ___ is nicer when Shug is around.

A 7. Why is Sofia in jail?
- A. The mayor's wife asked Sofia if she would like to be her maid and Sofia said, "Hell no." The mayor was offended and slapped Sofia. She punched the mayor and was thrown in jail.
- B. The store owner tries to cheat Sofia when she is buying cloth. She argues with him. He throws her out, keeping her money and not giving her any cloth. She bangs on the locked door and yells and is arrested for disrupting the peace.
- C. Sofia attacks Squeak when she sees her hugging Harpo. Harpo pulls Sofia off his girlfriend, and Sofia's date slugs Harpo for touching Sofia. The place gets so rowdy, the police arrive and Sofia is arrested with a number of others.
- D. Sofia is in town and begins to feel sick. She cannot find a Colored bathroom, so she sneaks into the white bathroom. On her way out, she gets caught by a shop owner who immediately calls the police.

B 8. What is the plan for getting Sofia out of jail?
- A. To try to make the case that Sofia is mentally unstable, getting her to a mental hospital or back home in the care of her family
- B. To tell the warden Sofia is happy in jail and the way to really punish her is to make her work for a white woman
- C. To get dynamite from the people building a nearby bridge and bust her out one night
- D. To ask for parole for good behavior, pleading for Sofia to be back with her six children and under house arrest

D 9. How do Celie and Shug get the rest of Nettie's letters without Albert's realizing they have them?
- A. Celie and Albert go to church while Shug goes through Albert's trunk to find the letters, later hiding them under Celie's pillow for her to read that night.
- B. Shug confronts Albert about the letter and refuses to speak to him ever again if he doesn't come clean with Celie and let her have her letters.
- C. Shug leaves the key for Celie while she takes Albert to the jukejoint for the night to get drunk, thinking Celie should have enough time to read most of the letters.
- D. Shug gets the keys to Albert's trunk. They steam open the envelopes, taking out the letters and putting the empty envelopes back in the trunk.

D 10. What does Celie discover about the two children she had with her father?
- A. Celie discovers her children are living with their father's aunt.
- B. Celie discovers her children are living in an orphanage outside of town.
- C. Celie discovers her children are dead.
- D. Celie discovers her children are alive and have been adopted by Samuel and Corrine.

C 11. What surprises Nettie about slavery?
- A. America wasn't the only country that had slaves.
- B. Slaves used to be severely beaten and many died from cruel treatment.
- C. That Africans used to capture their own people and sell them into the slave trade.
- D. People used to be auctioned off like cattle at town markets.

B 12. Why are the Olinka happy to see there is a road being built to their village? What later upsets them about the road?
- A. They are happy since it will allow for increased trade with neighboring villages, making survival in the rainy season much easier. They are later upset to learn they will have to pay a large fee to use the road, making trade nearly impossible.
- B. They are happy since it will make travel much quicker and easier to and from the village. They are later upset to learn the road is not stopping at their village but going straight through it and destroying several buildings.
- C. They are happy since it will finally allow for their village to have modern amenities like those found in larger cities. They are later upset to learn that the road is not sturdy enough to survive the rainy season and will be destroyed after only a few months of use.
- D. They are happy since it is providing work for many people of their village in a time when money is tight. They are later upset because the men do not pay them as promised, and the Olinka realize they worked hard for nothing in return.

B 13. Who does Corrine believe are Adam and Olivia's parents?
- A. Corrine believes Nettie and Mr. ____ are Adam and Olivia's birth parents.
- B. Corrine believes Nettie and Samuel are Adam and Olivia's birth parents.
- C. Corrine believes Celie and Albert are Adam and Olivia's birth parents.
- D. Corrine believes Celie and Samuel are Adam and Olivia's birth parents.

B 14. Why had Samuel urged Nettie to come to Africa?
- A. Samuel urged Nettie to come to Africa because he saw how close she and Olivia were and thought it would make the journey easier for Olivia.
- B. Samuel urged Nettie to come to Africa because he thought Adam and Olivia were Nettie's children, and he wanted them to be together.
- C. Samuel urged Nettie to come to Africa because he had fallen in love with her.
- D. Samuel urged Nettie to come to Africa because he knew Corrine would never be able to take care of the children.

B 15. Why doesn't Celie write to God anymore?
- A. Celie doesn't write to God anymore because she is writing to Shug.
- B. Celie doesn't write to God anymore because she thinks God is a man and all the men in her life are no-good and always let her down.
- C. Celie doesn't write to God anymore because she can now write to Nettie.
- D. Celie doesn't write to God anymore because she feels she is storng enough to handle her problems herself.

D 16. After moving to Memphis, what type of business does Celie start? What is the name of the business?
- A. Celie begins her own laundry business and she calls it "Cleanclothes, Unlimited."
- B. Celie begins her own pants business and she calls it "Pantsfolks, Unlimited."
- C. Celie begins her own laundry business and she calls it "Cleanfolks, Unlimited."
- D. Celie begins her own pants business and she calls it "Folkspants, Unlimited."

B 17. What does Celie learn about Mr. _____ and how he's been living since she moved away?
- A. Mr. _____ hired help for the fields and got a job in town working for the county jail. He makes enough money to live from his job and is creating a savings account with the money made off his land.
- B. Mr. _____ has been working very hard in the fields and keeping the house up nicely.
- C. Mr. _____ hired a young woman to live with him to help around the house and keep up with the cooking.
- D. Mr. _____'s older sister moved in with her three children after her husband was killed. Mr. _____ has been supporting the family for a few months now.

D 18. What happens to Nettie and Samuel's relationship when they travel to England?
- A. They grow closer in their friendship and decide to always stay in touch no matter what happens.
- B. They argue about whether or not to send the children to school in England or take them back to Africa and damage their friendship.
- C. They realize it is too hard to be friends without Corrine around and decide to go their separate ways.
- D. They realize their love for each other and get married.

B 19. What does Albert ask Celie? What is her response?
- A. He asks her to help him win back Shug. She says she loves Shug too and is trying to win her back herself.
- B. He asks her to marry him again, but this time in spirit and flesh. She says no and asks if they can just be friends.
- C. He asks her if she hates him for all the times he mistreated her over the years. She says she has finally forgiven him.
- D. He asks her if he can make shirts to go with her pants to sell them as sets. She says he can make shirts, but she won't sell them as part of her business.

A 20. Who is Celie reunited with at the end of the novel?
- A. Nettie, Olivia, and Adam
- B. Her mother
- C. Shug and her two children
- D. Her old school teacher

IV. Vocabulary

R	1.	HOSPITALITY	A.	Tiresome by reason of length, slowness, or dullness
N	2.	FRACTIOUS	B.	Strong distaste or objection
I	3.	VOUCH	C.	The act of banishing or excluding
L	4.	AFFLICTION	D.	Attitude of not caring one way or another
E	5.	DIGNITY	E.	Quality of being worthy of respect
P	6.	SERENE	F.	Defiant; shameless
H	7.	CONSCIENTIOUS	G.	Inborn; existing from birth
F	8.	BRAZEN	H.	Meticulously careful; dutiful
O	9.	APTITUDE	I.	Guarantee; certify; attest to
C	10.	OSTRACISM	J.	Taking another's possessions or rights gradually or stealthily
G	11.	INNATE	K.	Engrossed; had one's attention held
A	12.	TEDIOUS	L.	A condition of pain, suffering, or distress
M	13.	PIOUS	M.	Having or exhibiting religious reverence; devout
T	14.	RECLUSE	N.	Inclined to make trouble
J	15.	ENCROACHMENTS	O.	Capability; ability
K	16.	RIVETED	P.	Calm, peaceful, or tranquil
Q	17.	SOJOURN	Q.	A temporary stay
S	18.	NAIVE	R.	The treatment of guests and strangers in a warm, friendly, generous way
D	19.	INDIFFERENCE	S.	Lacking worldly experience and understanding; lacking sophistication
B	20.	REPUGNANCE	T.	A person who lives in seclusion or apart from society

The Color Purple Multiple Choice Unit Test 2

I. Matching

____ 1.	FATHER	A.	Mother of Olivia and Adam
____ 2.	DIAPER	B.	Mary Agnes
____ 3.	LETTERS	C.	The only piece of mail Albert ever gives Celie directly
____ 4.	SONG	D.	Celie's was lynched for running a successful business
____ 5.	PANTS	E.	Celie starts a business making these.
____ 6.	ROOFLEAF	F.	"Olivia" is embroidered on this.
____ 7.	SISTER	G.	Mr. ___ hides her letters from Celie.
____ 8.	QUILT	H.	Nettie uses this to remind Corrine she had once met the mother of Adam and Olivia.
____ 9.	PALLBEARER	I.	How Celie knows what is going on in Nettie's life
____ 10.	TELEGRAM	J.	Sofia fights with Harpo about being this.
____ 11.	SQUEAK	K.	She fights back when her husband beats her.
____ 12.	SHUG	L.	He reveals the true story about Nettie and Celie's father.
____ 13.	SOFIA	M.	Mr. ___
____ 14.	HARPO	N.	The Olinka worship it.
____ 15.	ALBERT	O.	Shug writes & sings this for Celie
____ 16.	CELIE	P.	Shug is in love with this 19 year-old musician.
____ 17.	NETTIE	Q.	Sofia's husband
____ 18.	SAMUEL	R.	Tashi's boyfriend
____ 19.	ADAM	S.	What Corrine would like Nettie to call her
____ 20.	GERMAINE	T.	Albert & Celie both love her.

II. Multiple Choice

1. How many times has Celie given birth? Who is the father?
   A. She has one child by the school teacher.
   B. She has three children by three different fathers.
   C. She has four children by the white man for whom her father works.
   D. She has two children by her father.

2. What kind of a business does Harpo start, and where does he open it?
   A. Harpo opens a brothel in his and Sofia's home.
   B. Harpo opens a jukejoint in his and Sofia's home.
   C. Harpo opens a meat-packing operation in his and Sofia's home.
   D. Harpo opens restaurant in his and Sofia's home.

3. Who is Squeak, and how did she lose two of her teeth?
   A. Squeak is Harpo's girlfriend. She was walking home from church when a white man pulled up in a car. He tried to take advantage of her, but she fought back, losing two teeth in the process.
   B. Squeak is Harpo's girlfriend. She talked back to Mr. _____ one night and he hit her, knocking out two of her teeth.
   C. Squeak is Harpo's girlfriend. She called Sofia a bitch and told her to stop dancing with her man. She then slapped Sofia, and Sofia punched her back, knocking out two of her teeth.
   D. Squeak is Harpo's girlfriend. She was singing at the jukejoint one night when Sofia hit her with a bottle, knocking out two of her teeth.

4. Why is Sofia in jail?
   A. Sofia attacks Squeak when she sees her hugging Harpo. Harpo pulls Sofia off his girlfriend, and Sofia's date slugs Harpo for touching Sofia. The place gets so rowdy, the police arrive and Sofia is arrested with a number of others.
   B. Sofia is in town and begins to feel sick. She cannot find a Colored bathroom, so she sneaks into the white bathroom. On her way out, she gets caught by a shop owner who immediately calls the police.
   C. The mayor's wife asked Sofia if she would like to be her maid and Sofia said, "Hell no." The mayor was offended and slapped Sofia. She punched the mayor and was thrown in jail.
   D. The store owner tries to cheat Sofia when she is buying cloth. She argues with him. He throws her out, keeping her money and not giving her any cloth. She bangs on the locked door and yells and is arrested for disrupting the peace.

5. How do Celie and Shug get the rest of Nettie's letters without Albert's realizing they have them?
   A. Shug gets the keys to Albert's trunk. They steam open the envelopes, taking out the letters and putting the empty envelopes back in the trunk.
   B. Celie and Albert go to church while Shug goes through Albert's trunk to find the letters, later hiding them under Celie's pillow for her to read that night.
   C. Shug confronts Albert about the letter and refuses to speak to him ever again if he doesn't come clean with Celie and let her have her letters.
   D. Shug leaves the key for Celie while she takes Albert to the jukejoint for the night to get drunk, thinking Celie should have enough time to read most of the letters.

6. What does Celie discover about the two children she had with her father?
   A. Celie discovers her children are living in an orphanage outside of town.
   B. Celie discovers her children are dead.
   C. Celie discovers her children are living with their father's aunt.
   D. Celie discovers her children are alive and have been adopted by Samuel and Corrine.

7. What does Shug teach Celie about God?
   A. Shug says God created sin and therefore doesn't mind if people stray from the right path everyone once in a while. She also says that God wants people to enjoy life and all He has created.
   B. She says God is for people who are dead or dying and the living should focus on living and experiencing the world. She also says religion is something created by white men, making it hard for her to believe.
   C. Shug tells Celie that God isn't a man or a woman, but an It. She tells Celie God is inside everyone, and they just have to find it.
   D. Shug tells Celie that God doesn't care about women and only listens to men. She also says that praying to Him each day and trying to live life for Him is ridiculous.

8. How are the Olinka people treated after the rubber factory is built?
   A. They are rewarded by the factory owners for giving up their land with gifts from the white world, like radios, bikes, jeans, mirrors, and toys. They are also paid for their time working in the factory and are permitted to live in the baracks provided.
   B. They are required to work for the factory, even though the conditions are poor and several people have been injured as a result of the dangerous work. They also are prohibited from practicing their tribal traditions and must adopt the ways of the white people.
   C. They are forced to move to a barren area of land that is without water six months of the year. In this time, they must pay the factory for water. There is also no more roofleaf left, leaving the Olinka people without their item of worship.
   D. They are given the opportunity to either work for the factory or continue to live on their land. They are permitted to use the resources of the factory and can make a nice living by trading with the factory owners. They are also allowed to retain their tribal traditions.

9. What reasons does Tashi give for refusing to marry Adam?
   A. She is worried Americans will look down on her because of the scarification marks on her face and her very dark skin. She is also worried Adam will find someone else to love in America, and she will then be left all alone.
   B. She is scared to leave the Olinka village and leave behind the customs and traditions she values. She is also scared Americans will think she is dumb since she is from Africa.
   C. She is already engaged to an Olinka tribal leader and feels obligated to honor her commitment. She is also fearful Adam will want children; she knows she is unable to reproduce after the female initiation ceremony.
   D. She is angry that Adam went to England and knows he will one day leave her again if it suits his own needs. She is also angry he waited so long to find her and feels this may be a sign he doesn't love her.

10. What does Adam do to prove his love and devotion to Tashi?
    A. Adam stays with Tashi in Africa.
    B. Adam goes through the Olinka male initiation ceremony.
    C. Adam has his faced scarred to look like Tashi's.
    D. Adam performs the Olinka marriage dance before the entire Olinka tribe.

III. Quotations: Explain the importance and meaning of the following quotations:

1. "Every time they ast me to do something, Miss Celie, I act like I'm you. I jump right up and do just what they say."

2. "I remember one time you said your life made you feel so ashamed you couldn't even talk about it to God, you had to write it, bad as you thought your writing was."

3. "I'm pore, I'm black, I may be ugly and can't cook, a voice say to everything listening. But I'm here."

4. "I start to wonder why us need love. Why us suffer. Why us black. Why us men and women. Where do children really come from. It didn't take long to realize I didn't hardly know nothing. And that if you ast yourself why you black or a man or a woman or a bush it don't mean nothing if you don't ask why you here, period...I think us here to wonder, myself. To wonder. To ast. And that in wondering bout the big things and asting bout the big things, you learn about the little ones, almost by accident. But you never know nothing more about the big things than you start out with. The more I wonder, he say, the more I love."

IV. Composition
1. How does Celie's view of God change over the course of the novel?

2. What is the significance of the title of the novel?

V. Vocabulary

____ 1. TRIFLING A. More than is needed

____ 2. SPITEFUL B. Desiring to harm, annoy, frustrate, or humiliate another person

____ 3. HAGGARD C. Bring to mind; recall

____ 4. OVERABUNDANT D. Rough and noisy; noisily jolly or rowdy

____ 5. INDUSTRIOUS E. Hard-working

____ 6. COVET F. An act of cursing or speaking against God

____ 7. REPARATIONS G. Amends for wrong or injury done

____ 8. IMMENSITIES H. Carry on despite hardships

____ 9. BLASPHEMY I. Loud howling, wailing, or lamenting

____ 10. MANIFEST J. Worthy of imitation as a good example

____ 11. ADRIFT K. Direct and straightforward

____ 12. CONJURE L. Vastness, boundlessness

____ 13. ULULATION M. Show or demonstrate plainly; reveal

____ 14. VERBOSITY N. Wordiness

____ 15. EXEMPLARY O. Wish for longingly

____ 16. BOISTEROUS P. Of chief concern or importance

____ 17. ENDURE Q. Without direction or purpose

____ 18. SABOTAGE R. Underhanded interference

____ 19. FORTHRIGHT S. Appearing worn and exhausted

____ 20. PARAMOUNT T. Of very little importance; trivial; insignificant

The Color Purple Multiple Choice Unit Test 2 Answer Key

I. Matching

D	1.	FATHER	A.	Mother of Olivia and Adam
F	2.	DIAPER	B.	Mary Agnes
I	3.	LETTERS	C.	The only piece of mail Albert ever gives Celie directly
O	4.	SONG	D.	Celie's was lynched for running a successful business
E	5.	PANTS	E.	Celie starts a business making these.
N	6.	ROOFLEAF	F.	"Olivia" is embroidered on this.
S	7.	SISTER	G.	Mr. ___ hides her letters from Celie.
H	8.	QUILT	H.	Nettie uses this to remind Corrine she had once met the mother of Adam and Olivia.
J	9.	PALLBEARER	I.	How Celie knows what is going on in Nettie's life
C	10.	TELEGRAM	J.	Sofia fights with Harpo about being this.
B	11.	SQUEAK	K.	She fights back when her husband beats her.
T	12.	SHUG	L.	He reveals the true story about Nettie and Celie's father.
K	13.	SOFIA	M.	Mr. ___
Q	14.	HARPO	N.	The Olinka worship it.
M	15.	ALBERT	O.	Shug writes & sings this for Celie
A	16.	CELIE	P.	Shug is in love with this 19 year-old musician.
G	17.	NETTIE	Q.	Sofia's husband
L	18.	SAMUEL	R.	Tashi's boyfriend
R	19.	ADAM	S.	What Corrine would like Nettie to call her
P	20.	GERMAINE	T.	Albert & Celie both love her.

II. Multiple Choice

D 1.   How many times has Celie given birth? Who is the father?
   A. She has one child by the school teacher.
   B. She has three children by three different fathers.
   C. She has four children by the white man for whom her father works.
   D. She has two children by her father.

B 2.   What kind of a business does Harpo start, and where does he open it?
   A. Harpo opens a brothel in his and Sofia's home.
   B. Harpo opens a jukejoint in his and Sofia's home.
   C. Harpo opens a meat-packing operation in his and Sofia's home.
   D. Harpo opens restaurant in his and Sofia's home.

C 3.   Who is Squeak, and how did she lose two of her teeth?
   A. Squeak is Harpo's girlfriend. She was walking home from church when a white man pulled up in a car. He tried to take advantage of her, but she fought back, losing two teeth in the process.
   B. Squeak is Harpo's girlfriend. She talked back to Mr. _____ one night and he hit her, knocking out two of her teeth.
   C. Squeak is Harpo's girlfriend. She called Sofia a bitch and told her to stop dancing with her man. She then slapped Sofia, and Sofia punched her back, knocking out two of her teeth.
   D. Squeak is Harpo's girlfriend. She was singing at the jukejoint one night when Sofia hit her with a bottle, knocking out two of her teeth.

C 4.   Why is Sofia in jail?
   A. Sofia attacks Squeak when she sees her hugging Harpo. Harpo pulls Sofia off his girlfriend, and Sofia's date slugs Harpo for touching Sofia. The place gets so rowdy, the police arrive and Sofia is arrested with a number of others.
   B. Sofia is in town and begins to feel sick. She cannot find a Colored bathroom, so she sneaks into the white bathroom. On her way out, she gets caught by a shop owner who immediately calls the police.
   C. The mayor's wife asked Sofia if she would like to be her maid and Sofia said, "Hell no." The mayor was offended and slapped Sofia. She punched the mayor and was thrown in jail.
   D. The store owner tries to cheat Sofia when she is buying cloth. She argues with him. He throws her out, keeping her money and not giving her any cloth. She bangs on the locked door and yells and is arrested for disrupting the peace.

A 5. How do Celie and Shug get the rest of Nettie's letters without Albert's realizing they have them?
- A. Shug gets the keys to Albert's trunk. They steam open the envelopes, taking out the letters and putting the empty envelopes back in the trunk.
- B. Celie and Albert go to church while Shug goes through Albert's trunk to find the letters, later hiding them under Celie's pillow for her to read that night.
- C. Shug confronts Albert about the letter and refuses to speak to him ever again if he doesn't come clean with Celie and let her have her letters.
- D. Shug leaves the key for Celie while she takes Albert to the jukejoint for the night to get drunk, thinking Celie should have enough time to read most of the letters.

D 6. What does Celie discover about the two children she had with her father?
- A. Celie discovers her children are living in an orphanage outside of town.
- B. Celie discovers her children are dead.
- C. Celie discovers her children are living with their father's aunt.
- D. Celie discovers her children are alive and have been adopted by Samuel and Corrine.

C 7. What does Shug teach Celie about God?
- A. Shug says God created sin and therefore doesn't mind if people stray from the right path everyone once in a while. She also says that God wants people to enjoy life and all He has created.
- B. She says God is for people who are dead or dying and the living should focus on living and experiencing the world. She also says religion is something created by white men, making it hard for her to believe.
- C. Shug tells Celie that God isn't a man or a woman, but an It. She tells Celie God is inside everyone, and they just have to find it.
- D. Shug tells Celie that God doesn't care about women and only listens to men. She also says that praying to Him each day and trying to live life for Him is ridiculous.

C 8. How are the Olinka people treated after the rubber factory is built?
   A. They are rewarded by the factory owners for giving up their land with gifts from the white world, like radios, bikes, jeans, mirrors, and toys. They are also paid for their time working in the factory and are permitted to live in the baracks provided.
   B. They are required to work for the factory, even though the conditions are poor and several people have been injured as a result of the dangerous work. They also are prohibited from practicing their tribal traditions and must adopt the ways of the white people.
   C. They are forced to move to a barren area of land that is without water six months of the year. In this time, they must pay the factory for water. There is also no more roofleaf left, leaving the Olinka people without their item of worship.
   D. They are given the opportunity to either work for the factory or continue to live on their land. They are permitted to use the resources of the factory and can make a nice living by trading with the factory owners. They are also allowed to retain their tribal traditions.

A 9. What reasons does Tashi give for refusing to marry Adam?
   A. She is worried Americans will look down on her because of the scarification marks on her face and her very dark skin. She is also worried Adam will find someone else to love in America, and she will then be left all alone.
   B. She is scared to leave the Olinka village and leave behind the customs and traditions she values. She is also scared Americans will think she is dumb since she is from Africa.
   C. She is already engaged to an Olinka tribal leader and feels obligated to honor her commitment. She is also fearful Adam will want children; she knows she is unable to reproduce after the female initiation ceremony.
   D. She is angry that Adam went to England and knows he will one day leave her again if it suits his own needs. She is also angry he waited so long to find her and feels this may be a sign he doesn't love her.

C 10. What does Adam do to prove his love and devotion to Tashi?
   A. Adam stays with Tashi in Africa.
   B. Adam goes through the Olinka male initiation ceremony.
   C. Adam has his faced scarred to look like Tashi's.
   D. Adam performs the Olinka marriage dance before the entire Olinka tribe.

V. Vocabulary

T	1.	TRIFLING	A.	More than is needed
B	2.	SPITEFUL	B.	Desiring to harm, annoy, frustrate, or humiliate another person
S	3.	HAGGARD	C.	Bring to mind; recall
A	4.	OVERABUNDANT	D.	Rough and noisy; noisily jolly or rowdy
E	5.	INDUSTRIOUS	E.	Hard-working
O	6.	COVET	F.	An act of cursing or speaking against God
G	7.	REPARATIONS	G.	Amends for wrong or injury done
L	8.	IMMENSITIES	H.	Carry on despite hardships
F	9.	BLASPHEMY	I.	Loud howling, wailing, or lamenting
M	10.	MANIFEST	J.	Worthy of imitation as a good example
Q	11.	ADRIFT	K.	Direct and straightforward
C	12.	CONJURE	L.	Vastness, boundlessness
I	13.	ULULATION	M.	Show or demonstrate plainly; reveal
N	14.	VERBOSITY	N.	Wordiness
J	15.	EXEMPLARY	O.	Wish for longingly
D	16.	BOISTEROUS	P.	Of chief concern or importance
H	17.	ENDURE	Q.	Without direction or purpose
R	18.	SABOTAGE	R.	Underhanded interference
K	19.	FORTHRIGHT	S.	Appearing worn and exhausted
P	20.	PARAMOUNT	T.	Of very little importance; trivial; insignificant

UNIT RESOURCE MATERIALS

BULLETIN BOARD IDEAS *The Color Purple*

1. Save one corner of the board for the best of students' *The Color Purple* writing assignments.
2. Take one of the word search puzzles from the extra activities packet and with a marker copy it over in a large size on the bulletin board. Write the clue words to find to one side. Invite students prior to and after class to find the words and circle them on the bulletin board.
3. Write several of the most significant quotations from the book onto the board on brightly colored paper.
4. Make a bulletin board listing the vocabulary words for this unit. As you complete sections of the novel and discuss the vocabulary for each section, write the definitions on the bulletin board. (If your board is one students face frequently, it will help them learn the words.)
5. Create a bulletin board with photos and information about African American history.
6. Create a bulletin board about the women's rights movement.
7. Make a bulletin board advertising other African American authors. Include a colorful cover for each book and a short tease to get students interested.
8. Create a bulletin board with scenes and posters from the movie and musical version on the novel.
9. Post recent media coverage of *The Color Purple*. Be sure to include interviews with the author and recent appearances around the country.
10. Create a KWL chart for the unit on the bulletin board with your students.
11. Create a bulletin board about censorship. Post lists of the most frequently banned books in the United States and use quotations about censorship to encourage your students to think about where they stand on the issue.

MORE ACTIVITIES *The Color Purple*

1. Have students research African American history. Guide them to pay specific attention to the time period immediately following slavery and the struggles the race has endured and overcome since that time.
2. Have students conduct more research on domestic abuse and the emotional toll it takes on those involved.
3. Have students chart the changes in marriage roles over the past century. Guide them to look at how male and female roles have changed over the course of this time.
4. Have students explore the entertainment of the time. Instruct them to research jukejoints and listen to music of popular African American artists of the time.
5. Since this novel is frequently censored and banned from schools, hold a debate with your class on whether or not *The Color Purple* should be taught in schools.
6. Have your students select a scene in the novel with a lot of action. Then, have them rewrite the scene in the form of a comic book using quotes from the text.
7. Since quilting and sewing are a large part of the novel, have your students make their own quilt. One suggestion is to have students use old t-shirts from their life and patch them together to make a quilt with memories from events, schools, and activities they have participated in.
8. Celie struggles with the feelings she has for Shug. Have your students research same sex relationships to identify with the struggle many encounter when becoming involved in a relationship with a member of the same sex. You may also want to have your students write a short reflection outlining the reasons this process can be difficult.
9. When Sofia is arrested she is treated with much more violence because of her race. Ask students to find examples of current cases where a person who was arrested was mistreated due to his or her race.
10. The characters in the story are able to forgive each other and provide support and strength to each other throughout the novel. Have your students write about a time they forgave someone and mended a relationship.
11. Celie's self image is defined for part of the novel by how others view her. Nettie's self image is also altered based on how the Olinka people regard her. Ask your students to write about how the perceptions of others can alter the way a person views his or herself.
12. Alice Walker creates very dynamic characters in her novel. No one character is "all bad" and often times the reader can relate to a character's inappropriate behaviors after learning about other events that happened in his or her life. Have your students select a character from the novel and rewrite part of the story from his or her perspective. Encourage your students to really attempt to explain the characters actions and personality from his or her point of view.
13. Celie uses writing as an outlet to help her deal with her life. Ask your students to write about what role writing plays in their life. Encourage them to think beyond the formal writing and think in terms of emailing, instant messaging, and notes as well.
14. The Olinka people don't like to acknowledge that they sold their own people into the slave trade many years ago. Ask your students to conduct research on how the slave trade operated in Africa. Have them share their findings by creating a poster of other project.

15. As Nettie travels she is introduced to new fashion. Have your students research the fashion of the time and create paper dolls to demonstrate the styles of the time. You may also want to encourage students to use the text to compare the styles of the time to what the Olinka were wearing. Students could also design paper dolls to show off what Celie and other characters wore in the novel.

16. Reading Assignment 4 mentions several historical names in regards to missionaries. Have your students select a missionary mentioned in the novel and write a biography on his or her life and accomplishments.

17. Have students explore the rituals practiced among small African tribes. Ask students to write a magazine article, similar to what one would see in National Geographic, teaching others about their selected culture. You may also want to have students explore the rituals discussed in the novel like scarification and female circumcision.

18. Celie learns a lot about God and religion over the course of her life. Ask students to select a religion and learn more about it. Have them create an informational brochure about the religion and share it with the class.

19. Shakespeare's *The Taming of the Shrew* examines the roles of women in marriage. Have your students read this short play and compare what Shakespeare was saying about gender and marriage to what Alice Walker was saying as she wrote her novel.

20. Alice Walker has a compainion novel for *The Color Purple* called *Possessing the Secret of Joy*. This novel is told from the perspective of Adam, Olivia, and Tashi years after the end of the novel. Have students read this book and write a relfection on what they thought about the lives these characters continued to lead after *The Color Purple* ended.

21. Ask your students to write a reflection on this unit. Tell them to talk specifically about assignments they enjoyed and assignments that should be changed. Use their feedback to help you determine how to teach this novel again.

22. Have your students create a MySpace of Facebook profile for one of the characters in the novel. Later, allow them to share their results with the class.

23. Have your students watch the movie version of the book and compare and contrast the two.

24. Have students design a new book cover (front and back and inside flaps) for *The Color Purple*.

25. Have students design a bulletin board (ready to be put up; not just sketched) for *The Color Purple*.

26. Have students write out the characters in the book and cast famous actors and actresses for an updated movie version of the novel. Instruct students to write a brief explanation as to why the actor/actress they selected would be perfect for the part.

27. Have students create a soundtrack for *The Color Purple*. Have students burn a cd of the songs, design a cd cover, and include a brief explanation as to why they selected each song.

28. Have students select a character from the book and complete the "I Am" poem from that character's point of view.

29. Have your students write a letter to the author. Use the guidelines for letter writing provided.

UNIT WORD LIST *The Color Purple*

No.	Word	Clue/Definition
1.	ADAM	Tashi's boyfriend
2.	ALBERT	Mr. ___
3.	AUNT	Nettie to Adam
4.	AVERY	Shug's last name
5.	BIG	What Celie calls herself when she is pregnant
6.	BUD	Mr. ___'s son
7.	CELIE	Mother of Olivia and Adam
8.	CORRINE	Adoptive mother of Olivia & Adam
9.	CRUMBLE	Celie tells Albert everything he touches will do this until he does right by her.
10.	CURSES	Celie does this to Albert as she is leaving him.
11.	DIAPER	"Olivia" is embroidered on this.
12.	EDUCATION	This is very important to Nettie.
13.	FACE	Location of Adam and Tashi's scarification marks
14.	FATHER	Celie's was lynched for running a successful business
15.	FIGHT	Celie is jealous of Sofia's strength to do this.
16.	FOLKSPANTS	___ Unlimited
17.	GERMAINE	Shug is in love with this 19 year-old musician.
18.	GIRLS	The Olinka do not allow them to go to school.
19.	GOD	Celie addresses the entries in the first half of the book Dear ___
20.	GRADY	Shug's big Christmas surprise
21.	HARPO	Sofia's husband
22.	JAIL	Sofia spent time there.
23.	JANE	Mayor's daughter: Eleanor ___
24.	JUKEJOINT	Harpo turns his house into one.
25.	KNIFE	Celie stabs Albert's hand with one.
26.	LETTERS	How Celie knows what is going on in Nettie's life
27.	MARRY	What Samuel and Nettie do while in England
28.	MAYOR	Sofia punches this person and is thrown in jail.
29.	MILLIE	She insisted on Sofia's riding with her.
30.	MISSIONARY	Nettie travels to Africa to work as one.
31.	MOTHER	Celie to Olivia
32.	NETTIE	Mr. ___ hides her letters from Celie.
33.	OLIVIA	Celie's daughter
34.	PALLBEARER	Sofia fights with Harpo about being this.
35.	PANTS	Celie starts a business making these.
36.	PAULINE	Olivia
37.	QUILT	Nettie uses this to remind Corrine she had once met the mother of Adam and Olivia.

No.	Word	Clue/Definition
38.	REEFER	Grady's crop
39.	REVEREND	Samuel's occupation
40.	ROAD	The Olinka people are very excited about this being built.
41.	ROOFLEAF	The Olinka worship it.
42.	RUBBER	Kind of factory that forces the Olinka off their land
43.	SAMUEL	He reveals the true story about Nettie and Celie's father.
44.	SHAVING	Celie thinks about killing her husband while she is doing this for him.
45.	SHUG	Albert & Celie both love her.
46.	SISTER	What Corrine would like Nettie to call her
47.	SOFIA	She fights back when her husband beats her.
48.	SONG	Shug writes & sings this for Celie
49.	SPOUSE	Celie's relationship to Albert
50.	SQUEAK	Mary Agnes
51.	STORE	Celie inherits the house, land, and this from her father.
52.	TASHI	She undergoes a female initiation ceremony.
53.	TEETH	Sofia knocked out 2 of Squeak's.
54.	TELEGRAM	The only piece of mail Albert ever gives Celie directly
55.	TENNESSEE	Where Shug takes Celie
56.	WARDEN	He rapes Squeak.
57.	WATER	Olinkas have to pay for this.
58.	WHITE	Nettie feels other missionaries have been unsuccessful because they were __.
59.	WIFE	Corrine to Samuel
60.	YAMS	Used to cure Henrietta's sickness

WORD SEARCH - The Color Purple

```
G R A D Y T R P S A G M J A I L W H I T E
N E L C F E E A O V W A I C V R R F W E Y
I D L E A E E N N E T D S L Z E E O A N G
V U S L C T F T G R S A S M L N R L R N T
A C T I E H E S R Y E T K D J I A K D E G
H A R E S T R E B N K A O P U A E S E S B
S T E U L T H F I P E S H R K M B P N S B
Y I B V M T E L I U D H D U E R L A L E Y
Y O L R A B U R Q G L I P B J E L N E E Z
F N A F N A L S K J H G P B O G A T T R D
H K Z X P N H E J Z B T E E I M P S T E P
O L I V I A F G N Y P N Q R N A Y V E V C
W K W F D D H T T Q I M Z X T R G W R E R
Q Y R Z B M N L X R R I Z S R G Y N S R F
Z M O T H E R C R J J S L A M E Z S Z E S
R J O C G Q S O E S X S M K N L F N N N Y
Y T F Z U J C Y S T G I Q J S E M R L D Y
M Q L P Q R P W U W G O C P O T T E C G A
J C E S U M S Z O G R N R O F W U I G U M
B Z A E I A Y E P P I A P O I M A T N H L
Y T F Z L Y A M S L D R E P A I D T P S J
B I D Q T O C V D O A Y L S S D B E E Q S
W J A N E R B I G H B U D S E F I N K R H
```

ADAM	FACE	KNIFE	QUILT	SPOUSE
ALBERT	FATHER	LETTERS	REEFER	SQUEAK
AUNT	FIGHT	MARRY	REVEREND	STORE
AVERY	FOLKSPANTS	MAYOR	ROAD	TASHI
BIG	GERMAINE	MILLIE	ROOFLEAF	TEETH
BUD	GIRLS	MISSIONARY	RUBBER	TELEGRAM
CELIE	GOD	MOTHER	SAMUEL	TENNESSEE
CORRINE	GRADY	NETTIE	SHAVING	WARDEN
CRUMBLE	HARPO	OLIVIA	SHUG	WATER
CURSES	JAIL	PALLBEARER	SISTER	WHITE
DIAPER	JANE	PANTS	SOFIA	WIFE
EDUCATION	JUKEJOINT	PAULINE	SONG	YAMS

WORD SEARCH ANSWER KEY - The Color Purple

ADAM	FACE	KNIFE	QUILT	SPOUSE
ALBERT	FATHER	LETTERS	REEFER	SQUEAK
AUNT	FIGHT	MARRY	REVEREND	STORE
AVERY	FOLKSPANTS	MAYOR	ROAD	TASHI
BIG	GERMAINE	MILLIE	ROOFLEAF	TEETH
BUD	GIRLS	MISSIONARY	RUBBER	TELEGRAM
CELIE	GOD	MOTHER	SAMUEL	TENNESSEE
CORRINE	GRADY	NETTIE	SHAVING	WARDEN
CRUMBLE	HARPO	OLIVIA	SHUG	WATER
CURSES	JAIL	PALLBEARER	SISTER	WHITE
DIAPER	JANE	PANTS	SOFIA	WIFE
EDUCATION	JUKEJOINT	PAULINE	SONG	YAMS

CROSSWORD - The Color Purple

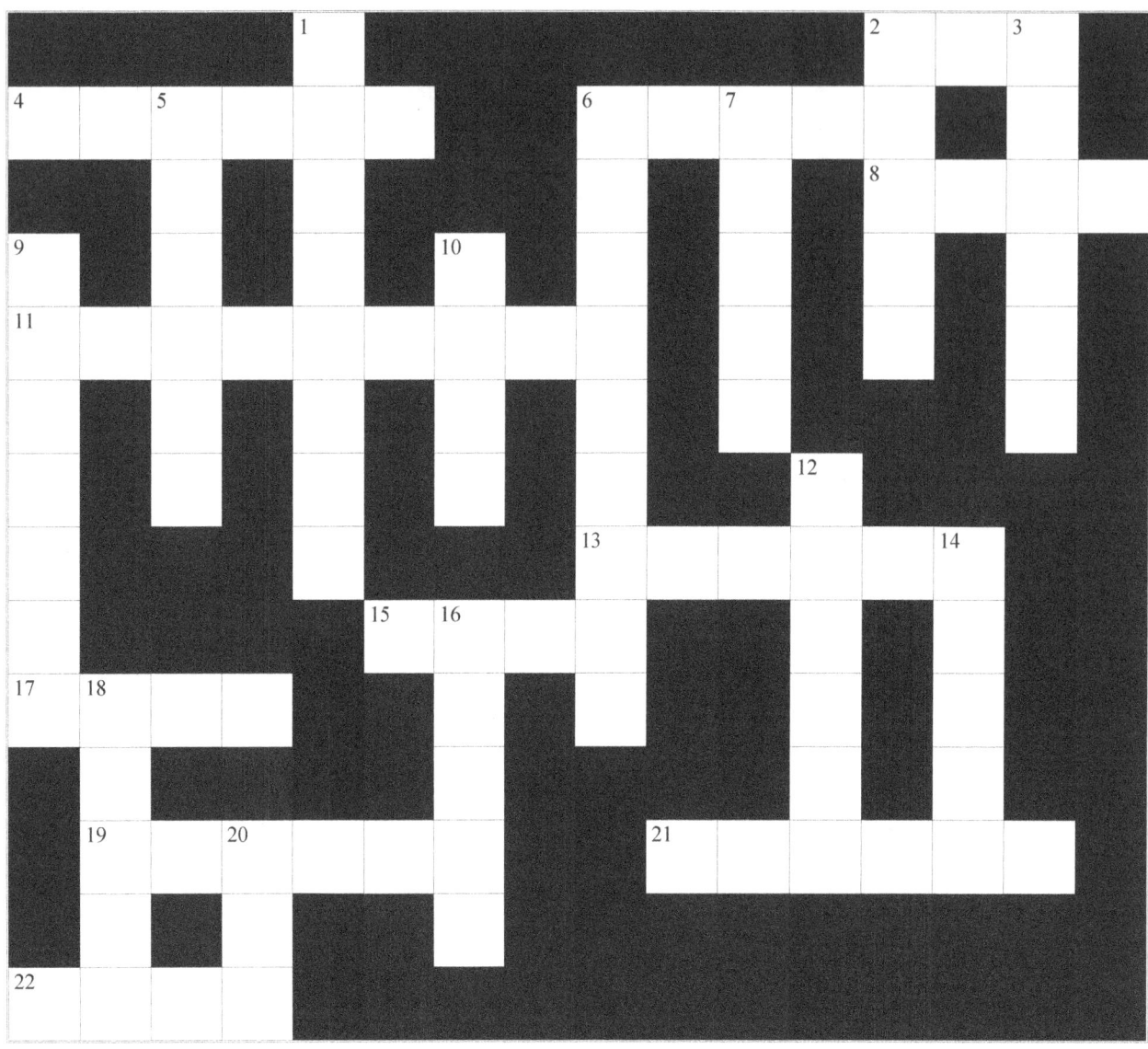

Across
2. Celie addresses the entries in the first half of the book to Dear ___
4. What Corrine would like Nettie to call her
6. She undergoes a female initiation ceremony.
8. The Olinka people are very excited about this being built.
11. This is very important to Nettie.
13. Mary Agnes
15. Mayor's daughter: Eleanor ___
17. Albert & Celie both love her.
19. Kind of factory that forces the Olinka off their land
21. Celie does this to Albert as she is leaving him.
22. Shug writes & sings this for Celie.

Down
1. Shug is in love with this 19 year-old musician.
2. The Olinka do not allow them to go to school.
3. Olivia's name is embroidered on this.
5. Celie's relationship to Albert
6. Where Shug takes Celie
7. She fights back when her husband beats her.
9. How Celie knows what is going on in Nettie's life
10. Corrine to Samuel
12. Grady's crop
14. Celie stabs Albert's hand with one.
16. Shug's last name
18. Sofia's husband
20. What Celie calls herself when she is pregnant

CROSSWORD ANSWER KEY - The Color Purple

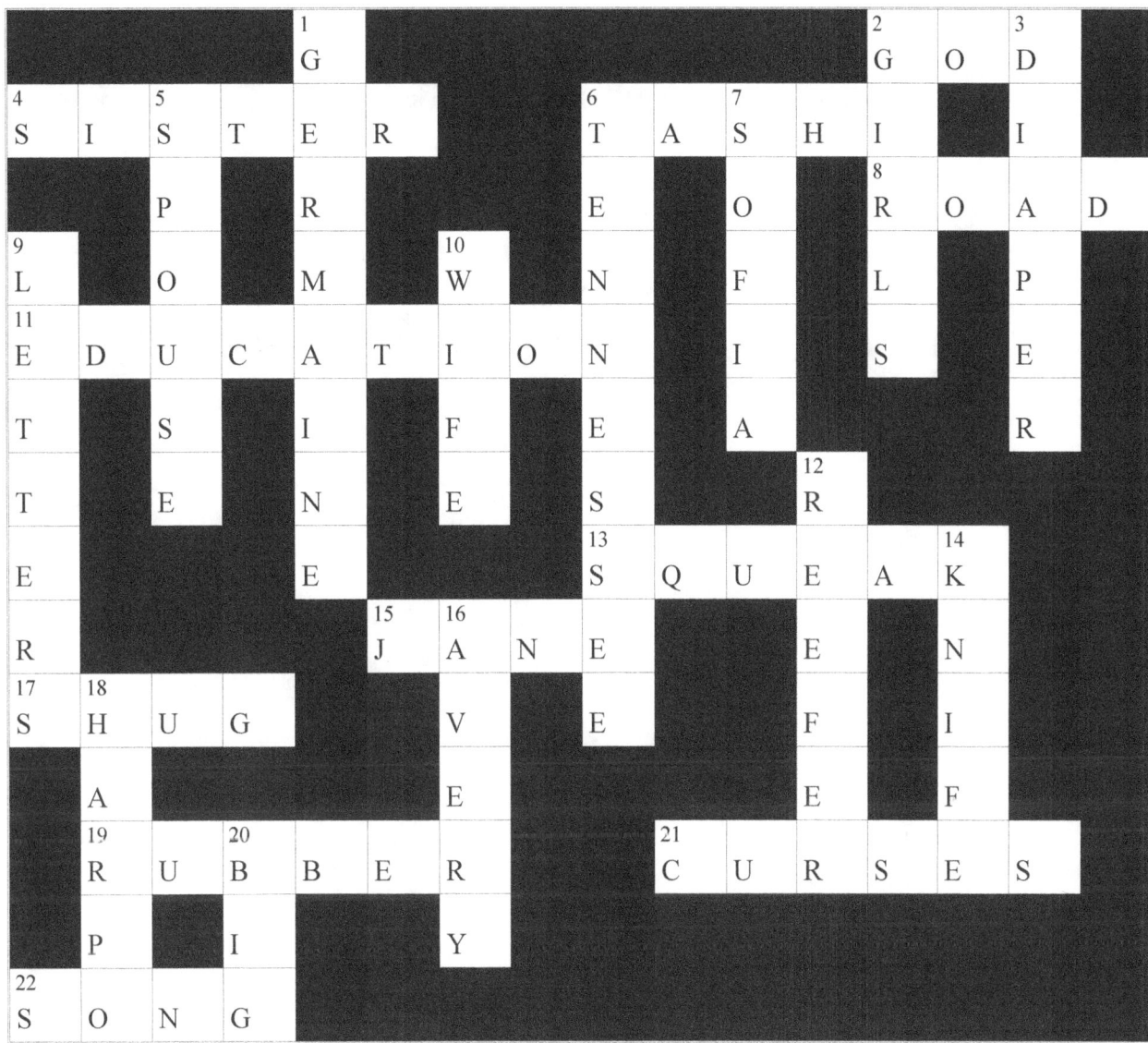

Across
2. Celie addresses the entries in the first half of the book to Dear ___
4. What Corrine would like Nettie to call her
6. She undergoes a female initiation ceremony.
8. The Olinka people are very excited about this being built.
11. This is very important to Nettie.
13. Mary Agnes
15. Mayor's daughter: Eleanor ___
17. Albert & Celie both love her.
19. Kind of factory that forces the Olinka off their land
21. Celie does this to Albert as she is leaving him.
22. Shug writes & sings this for Celie.

Down
1. Shug is in love with this 19 year-old musician.
2. The Olinka do not allow them to go to school.
3. Olivia's name is embroidered on this.
5. Celie's relationship to Albert
6. Where Shug takes Celie
7. She fights back when her husband beats her.
9. How Celie knows what is going on in Nettie's life
10. Corrine to Samuel
12. Grady's crop
14. Celie stabs Albert's hand with one.
16. Shug's last name
18. Sofia's husband
20. What Celie calls herself when she is pregnant

MATCHING 1 *The Color Purple*

____ 1. GERMAINE   A. The Olinka worship it.

____ 2. QUILT   B. Celie's daughter

____ 3. WIFE   C. She fights back when her husband beats her.

____ 4. ROOFLEAF   D. Celie thinks about killing her husband while she is doing this for him.

____ 5. WHITE   E. Shug is in love with this 19 year-old musician.

____ 6. SHAVING   F. Celie addresses the entries in the first half of the book Dear ___

____ 7. SONG   G. Nettie feels other missionaries have been unsuccessful because they were __.

____ 8. LETTERS   H. Mary Agnes

____ 9. BIG   I. How Celie knows what is going on in Nettie's life

____ 10. PALLBEARER   J. Mr. ___ hides her letters from Celie.

____ 11. TELEGRAM   K. Corrine to Samuel

____ 12. OLIVIA   L. Used to cure Henrietta's sickness

____ 13. CORRINE   M. What Celie calls herself when she is pregnant

____ 14. NETTIE   N. Sofia fights with Harpo about being this.

____ 15. ALBERT   O. The only piece of mail Albert ever gives Celie directly

____ 16. SOFIA   P. Nettie uses this to remind Corrine she had once met the mother of Adam and Olivia.

____ 17. SQUEAK   Q. Adoptive mother of Olivia & Adam

____ 18. YAMS   R. Location of Adam and Tashi's scarification marks

____ 19. FACE   S. Mr. ___

____ 20. GOD   T. Shug writes & sings this for Celie

MATCHING 1 ANSWER KEY *The Color Purple*

E	1.	GERMAINE	A.	The Olinka worship it.
P	2.	QUILT	B.	Celie's daughter
K	3.	WIFE	C.	She fights back when her husband beats her.
A	4.	ROOFLEAF	D.	Celie thinks about killing her husband while she is doing this for him.
G	5.	WHITE	E.	Shug is in love with this 19 year-old musician.
D	6.	SHAVING	F.	Celie addresses the entries in the first half of the book Dear ___
T	7.	SONG	G.	Nettie feels other missionaries have been unsuccessful because they were ___.
I	8.	LETTERS	H.	Mary Agnes
M	9.	BIG	I.	How Celie knows what is going on in Nettie's life
N	10.	PALLBEARER	J.	Mr. ___ hides her letters from Celie.
O	11.	TELEGRAM	K.	Corrine to Samuel
B	12.	OLIVIA	L.	Used to cure Henrietta's sickness
Q	13.	CORRINE	M.	What Celie calls herself when she is pregnant
J	14.	NETTIE	N.	Sofia fights with Harpo about being this.
S	15.	ALBERT	O.	The only piece of mail Albert ever gives Celie directly
C	16.	SOFIA	P.	Nettie uses this to remind Corrine she had once met the mother of Adam and Olivia.
H	17.	SQUEAK	Q.	Adoptive mother of Olivia & Adam
L	18.	YAMS	R.	Location of Adam and Tashi's scarification marks
R	19.	FACE	S.	Mr. ___
F	20.	GOD	T.	Shug writes & sings this for Celie

MATCHING 2 *The Color Purple*

____ 1. GRADY   A. Celie does this to Albert as she is leaving him.
____ 2. CURSES   B. She undergoes a female initiation ceremony.
____ 3. TENNESSEE   C. Albert & Celie both love her.
____ 4. GIRLS   D. The Olinka people are very excited about this being built.
____ 5. PANTS   E. Sofia's husband
____ 6. MISSIONARY   F. Harpo turns his house into one.
____ 7. MAYOR   G. Celie's was lynched for running a successful business
____ 8. JUKEJOINT   H. Shug's big Christmas surprise
____ 9. DIAPER   I. Where Shug takes Celie
____ 10. REEFER   J. What Samuel and Nettie do while in England
____ 11. MARRY   K. He reveals the true story about Nettie and Celie's father.
____ 12. TASHI   L. Nettie travels to Africa to work as one.
____ 13. ADAM   M. Mother of Olivia and Adam
____ 14. SAMUEL   N. Celie inherits the house, land, and this from her father.
____ 15. CELIE   O. Grady's crop
____ 16. HARPO   P. Sofia punches this person and is thrown in jail.
____ 17. SHUG   Q. The Olinka do not allow them to go to school.
____ 18. STORE   R. "Olivia" is embroidered on this.
____ 19. ROAD   S. Tashi's boyfriend
____ 20. FATHER   T. Celie starts a business making these.

MATCHING 2 ANSWER KEY *The Color Purple*

H	1.	GRADY	A.	Celie does this to Albert as she is leaving him.
A	2.	CURSES	B.	She undergoes a female initiation ceremony.
I	3.	TENNESSEE	C.	Albert & Celie both love her.
Q	4.	GIRLS	D.	The Olinka people are very excited about this being built.
T	5.	PANTS	E.	Sofia's husband
L	6.	MISSIONARY	F.	Harpo turns his house into one.
P	7.	MAYOR	G.	Celie's was lynched for running a successful business
F	8.	JUKEJOINT	H.	Shug's big Christmas surprise
R	9.	DIAPER	I.	Where Shug takes Celie
O	10.	REEFER	J.	What Samuel and Nettie do while in England
J	11.	MARRY	K.	He reveals the true story about Nettie and Celie's father.
B	12.	TASHI	L.	Nettie travels to Africa to work as one.
S	13.	ADAM	M.	Mother of Olivia and Adam
K	14.	SAMUEL	N.	Celie inherits the house, land, and this from her father.
M	15.	CELIE	O.	Grady's crop
E	16.	HARPO	P.	Sofia punches this person and is thrown in jail.
C	17.	SHUG	Q.	The Olinka do not allow them to go to school.
N	18.	STORE	R.	"Olivia" is embroidered on this.
D	19.	ROAD	S.	Tashi's boyfriend
G	20.	FATHER	T.	Celie starts a business making these.

JUGGLE LETTERS 1 *The Color Purple*

_____ = 1. GEMIENAR
Shug is in love with this 19 year-old musician.

_____ = 2. EVEDNRRE
Samuel's occupation

_____ = 3. LAPNIUE
Olivia

_____ = 4. ETELTRS
How Celie knows what is going on in Nettie's life

_____ = 5. EJTIUJNOK
Harpo turns his house into one.

_____ = 6. HGINVSA
Celie thinks about killing her husband while she is doing this for him.

_____ = 7. YIRMANSOIS
Nettie travels to Africa to work as one.

_____ = 8. TENSNSEEE
Where Shug takes Celie

_____ = 9. PRRALBELEA
Sofia fights with Harpo about being this.

_____ = 10. EERAMTLG
The only piece of mail Albert ever gives Celie directly

_____ = 11. YMARR
What Samuel and Nettie do while in England

_____ = 12. QUEASK
Mary Agnes

_____ = 13. UGSH
Albert & Celie both love her.

_____ = 14. ICROREN
Adoptive mother of Olivia & Adam

_____ = 15. LTAPSFNSKO
___ Unlimited

JUGGLE LETTERS 1 ANSWER KEY *The Color Purple*

GERMAINE	= 1.	GEMIENAR
		Shug is in love with this 19 year-old musician.
REVEREND	= 2.	EVEDNRRE
		Samuel's occupation
PAULINE	= 3.	LAPNIUE
		Olivia
LETTERS	= 4.	ETELTRS
		How Celie knows what is going on in Nettie's life
JUKEJOINT	= 5.	EJTIUJNOK
		Harpo turns his house into one.
SHAVING	= 6.	HGINVSA
		Celie thinks about killing her husband while she is doing this for him.
MISSIONARY	= 7.	YIRMANSOIS
		Nettie travels to Africa to work as one.
TENNESSEE	= 8.	TENSNSEEE
		Where Shug takes Celie
PALLBEARER	= 9.	PRRALBELEA
		Sofia fights with Harpo about being this.
TELEGRAM	= 10.	EERAMTLG
		The only piece of mail Albert ever gives Celie directly
MARRY	= 11.	YMARR
		What Samuel and Nettie do while in England
SQUEAK	= 12.	QUEASK
		Mary Agnes
SHUG	= 13.	UGSH
		Albert & Celie both love her.
CORRINE	= 14.	ICROREN
		Adoptive mother of Olivia & Adam
FOLKSPANTS	= 15.	LTAPSFNSKO
		___ Unlimited

JUGGLE LETTERS 2 *The Color Purple*

_____ = 1. DRAGY
Shug's big Christmas surprise

_____ = 2. MOARY
Sofia punches this person and is thrown in jail.

_____ = 3. AORFOEFL
The Olinka worship it.

_____ = 4. NESSETNEE
Where Shug takes Celie

_____ = 5. LTQIU
Nettie uses this to remind Corrine she had once met the mother of Adam and Olivia.

_____ = 6. BALLEPRRAE
Sofia fights with Harpo about being this.

_____ = 7. RFREEE
Grady's crop

_____ = 8. MSAY
Used to cure Henrietta's sickness

_____ = 9. AIFSO
She fights back when her husband beats her.

_____ = 10. HAROP
Sofia's husband

_____ = 11. TTINEE
Mr. ___ hides her letters from Celie.

_____ = 12. SLEMAU
He reveals the true story about Nettie and Celie's father.

_____ = 13. IOILAV
Celie's daughter

_____ = 14. TASHI
She undergoes a female initiation ceremony.

_____ = 15. PADIRE
"Olivia" is embroidered on this.

JUGGLE LETTERS 2 ANSWER KEY *The Color Purple*

GRADY	= 1.	DRAGY
		Shug's big Christmas surprise
MAYOR	= 2.	MOARY
		Sofia punches this person and is thrown in jail.
ROOFLEAF	= 3.	AORFOEFL
		The Olinka worship it.
TENNESSEE	= 4.	NESSETNEE
		Where Shug takes Celie
QUILT	= 5.	LTQIU
		Nettie uses this to remind Corrine she had once met the mother of Adam and Olivia.
PALLBEARER	= 6.	BALLEPRRAE
		Sofia fights with Harpo about being this.
REEFER	= 7.	RFREEE
		Grady's crop
YAMS	= 8.	MSAY
		Used to cure Henrietta's sickness
SOFIA	= 9.	AIFSO
		She fights back when her husband beats her.
HARPO	= 10.	HAROP
		Sofia's husband
NETTIE	= 11.	TTINEE
		Mr. ___ hides her letters from Celie.
SAMUEL	= 12.	SLEMAU
		He reveals the true story about Nettie and Celie's father.
OLIVIA	= 13.	IOILAV
		Celie's daughter
TASHI	= 14.	TASHI
		She undergoes a female initiation ceremony.
DIAPER	= 15.	PADIRE
		"Olivia" is embroidered on this.

VOCABULARY RESOURCE MATERIALS

The Color Purple Vocabulary

No.	Word	Clue/Definition
1.	ADRIFT	Without direction or purpose
2.	AFFLICTION	A condition of pain, suffering, or distress
3.	ALBINOS	People or animals with abnormally pale skin & hair
4.	APTITUDE	Capability; ability
5.	BEFELL	Happened or occurred
6.	BLASPHEMY	An act of cursing or speaking against God
7.	BOISTEROUS	Rough and noisy; noisily jolly or rowdy
8.	BRAZEN	Defiant; shameless
9.	CACKLE	Laugh in a shrill, broken manner
10.	CHIFFEROBE	Type of furniture having both drawers and space for hanging clothes
11.	COMMENCE	Begin; start
12.	CONCLUDE	Bring to an end; finish
13.	CONCOCTED	Prepared by mixing ingredients
14.	CONJURE	Bring to mind; recall
15.	CONSCIENTIOUS	Meticulously careful; dutiful
16.	COVET	Wish for longingly
17.	CULTIVATE	Prepare land for raising crops
18.	DIGNITY	Quality of being worthy of respect
19.	DOTE	Show excessive fondness or love
20.	DOWNTRODDEN	Oppressed; trampled upon
21.	DROVES	Large crowds of human beings
22.	ENCROACHMENTS	Taking another's possessions or rights gradually or stealthily
23.	ENDURE	Carry on despite hardships
24.	EXEMPLARY	Worthy of imitation as a good example
25.	FLOURISH	Thrive; grow or do well
26.	FORTHRIGHT	Direct and straightforward
27.	FRACTIOUS	Inclined to make trouble
28.	FRETTING	Worrying
29.	GLUTTONS	People who eat or consume immoderate amounts of food
30.	GRIM	Uninviting; stern; harsh
31.	HAGGARD	Appearing worn and exhausted
32.	HOSPITALITY	The treatment of guests and strangers in a warm, friendly, generous way
33.	IMMENSITIES	Vastness, boundlessness
34.	IMPISH	Mischievous
35.	INDIFFERENCE	Attitude of not caring one way or another
36.	INDUSTRIOUS	Hard-working
37.	INNATE	Inborn; existing from birth
38.	INTENT	Having the attention sharply focused or fixed on something

No.	Word	Clue/Definition
39.	LAVISH	Give or bestow in abundance; shower
40.	LUMINOUS	Radiating or reflecting light; shining; bright
41.	LYNCH	Put to death by hanging, by mob action, and without legal authority
42.	MANIFEST	Show or demonstrate plainly; reveal
43.	NAIVE	Lacking worldly experience and understanding; lacking sophistication
44.	NOTION	Idea
45.	OSTRACISM	The act of banishing or excluding
46.	OVERABUNDANT	More than is needed
47.	PARAMOUNT	Of chief concern or importance
48.	PIOUS	Having or exhibiting religious reverence; devout
49.	PREEN	Take pride or satisfaction in oneself; gloat
50.	PROCESSION	A group of persons, vehicles, or objects moving along in an orderly, formal manner
51.	RECLUSE	A person who lives in seclusion or apart from society
52.	REPARATIONS	Amends for wrong or injury done
53.	REPENT	Feel such sorrow for sin or fault as to change one's life for the better
54.	REPUGNANCE	Strong distaste or objection
55.	RESEMBLANCE	Similarity in appearance
56.	RIVETED	Engrossed; had one's attention held
57.	RUMMAGE	Search thoroughly by handling, turning over, or disarranging contents
58.	SABOTAGE	Underhanded interference
59.	SANCTIFIED	Made holy
60.	SCURRY	Move quickly or in haste; scamper
61.	SEINING	Large fishing net made to hang vertically in the water by weights at the lower edge and floats at the top
62.	SERENE	Calm, peaceful, or tranquil
63.	SOJOURN	A temporary stay
64.	SOMBER	Gloomy, dark, depressing, extremely serious
65.	SPITEFUL	Desiring to harm, annoy, frustrate, or humiliate another person
66.	STOUT	Bulky in figure; heavily built
67.	STRUMPET	Prostitute
68.	SULK	Remain silent or hold oneself aloof in an ill-humored or offended mood
69.	TEDIOUS	Tiresome by reason of length, slowness, or dullness
70.	TRIFLING	Of very little importance; trivial; insignificant
71.	ULULATION	Loud howling, wailing, or lamenting
72.	VERBOSITY	Wordiness
73.	VOUCH	Guarantee; certify; attest to

No.	Word	Clue/Definition
74.	WEARY	Tired

VOCABULARY WORD SEARCH - The Color Purple

```
G N I N I E S A B O T A G E D U T I T P A
L B C R O P U T R I F L I N G E N M P E S
U L O E F T O F O C V W P M P N U M X P A
T A N P L I I G R U R E B M O S O E P I N
T S C A O N T O K E T T U F Q M M N L O C
O P O R U D N L N X T R V E Y P A S U U T
N H C A R U E Y Z X T T D T L B R I M S I
S E T T I S I N X S P U I A G R A T I C F
D M E I S T C C X F L S R N X A P I N H I
I Y D O H R S H W C O Y T R G Z X E O Z E
G P I N S I N X N B G D F Z N E V S U L D
N C M S L O O R X R R D E Q N P T S C E
I X P N N U C E W A A S X Z N I W Q E D T
T L I M R S V M G C G T Q W T D E S R D A
Y A S Y U V K G T W X E D A H G U Y E C V
B V H R O L A I V E Y D L C A H K R N A I
E I B E J H O M M A V I U M O R Y D E C T
T S K C O U Y P I R T O M Z E V E R T K L
A H T L S C U R R Y V U S P I T E F U L U
N N B U Y D B S G E R S E N E V I T E E C
N N M S H C O G U Q E N K V I R W F X T T
I N T E N T C T F L T N I A D S E V O R D
E C N A N G U P E R K R N A L B I N O S R
```

ADRIFT	ENDURE	LUMINOUS	SCURRY
ALBINOS	EXEMPLARY	LYNCH	SEINING
APTITUDE	FLOURISH	NAIVE	SERENE
BEFELL	FRACTIOUS	NOTION	SOJOURN
BLASPHEMY	FRETTING	PARAMOUNT	SOMBER
BRAZEN	GLUTTONS	PIOUS	SPITEFUL
CACKLE	GRIM	PREEN	STOUT
CONCLUDE	HAGGARD	RECLUSE	STRUMPET
CONCOCTED	HOSPITALITY	REPARATIONS	SULK
CONSCIENTIOUS	IMMENSITIES	REPENT	TEDIOUS
COVET	IMPISH	REPUGNANCE	TRIFLING
CULTIVATE	INDUSTRIOUS	RIVETED	VERBOSITY
DIGNITY	INNATE	RUMMAGE	VOUCH
DOTE	INTENT	SABOTAGE	WEARY
DROVES	LAVISH	SANCTIFIED	

VOCABULARY WORD SEARCH ANSWER KEY - The Color Purple

ADRIFT	ENDURE	LUMINOUS	SCURRY
ALBINOS	EXEMPLARY	LYNCH	SEINING
APTITUDE	FLOURISH	NAIVE	SERENE
BEFELL	FRACTIOUS	NOTION	SOJOURN
BLASPHEMY	FRETTING	PARAMOUNT	SOMBER
BRAZEN	GLUTTONS	PIOUS	SPITEFUL
CACKLE	GRIM	PREEN	STOUT
CONCLUDE	HAGGARD	RECLUSE	STRUMPET
CONCOCTED	HOSPITALITY	REPARATIONS	SULK
CONSCIENTIOUS	IMMENSITIES	REPENT	TEDIOUS
COVET	IMPISH	REPUGNANCE	TRIFLING
CULTIVATE	INDUSTRIOUS	RIVETED	VERBOSITY
DIGNITY	INNATE	RUMMAGE	VOUCH
DOTE	INTENT	SABOTAGE	WEARY
DROVES	LAVISH	SANCTIFIED	

VOCABULARY CROSSWORD - The Color Purple

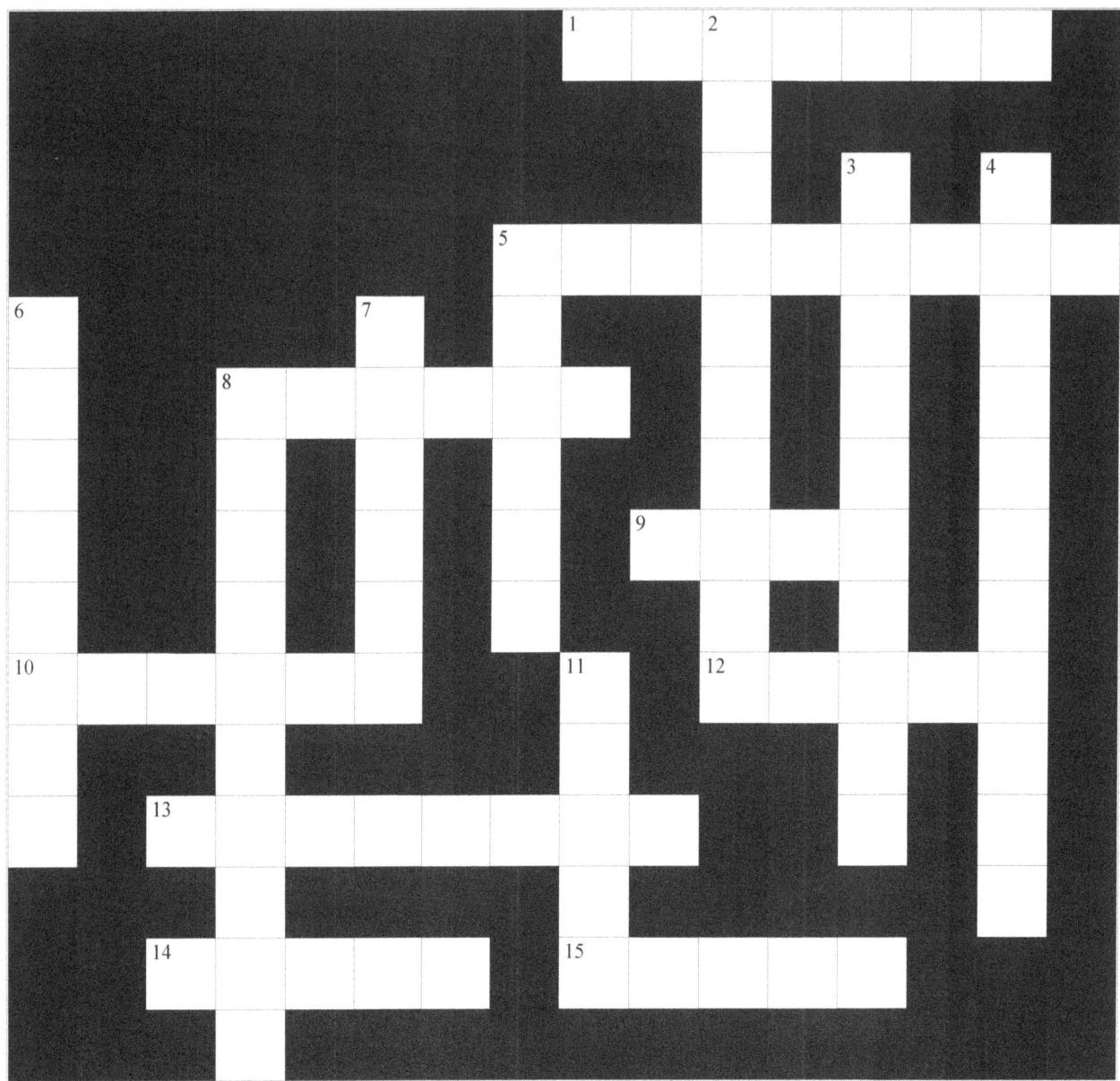

Across
1. People or animals with abnormally pale skin & hair
5. An act of cursing or speaking against God
8. Without direction or purpose
9. Show excessive fondness or love
10. Idea
12. Bulky in figure; heavily built
13. Prostitute
14. Wish for longingly
15. Lacking worldly experience and understanding; lacking sophistication

Down
2. Rough and noisy; noisily jolly or rowdy
3. Type of furniture having both drawers and space for hanging clothes
4. Vastness, boundlessness
5. Happened or occurred
6. Begin; start
7. Defiant; shameless
8. A condition of pain, suffering, or distress
11. Take pride or satisfaction in oneself; gloat

VOCABULARY CROSSWORD ANSWER KEY - The Color Purple

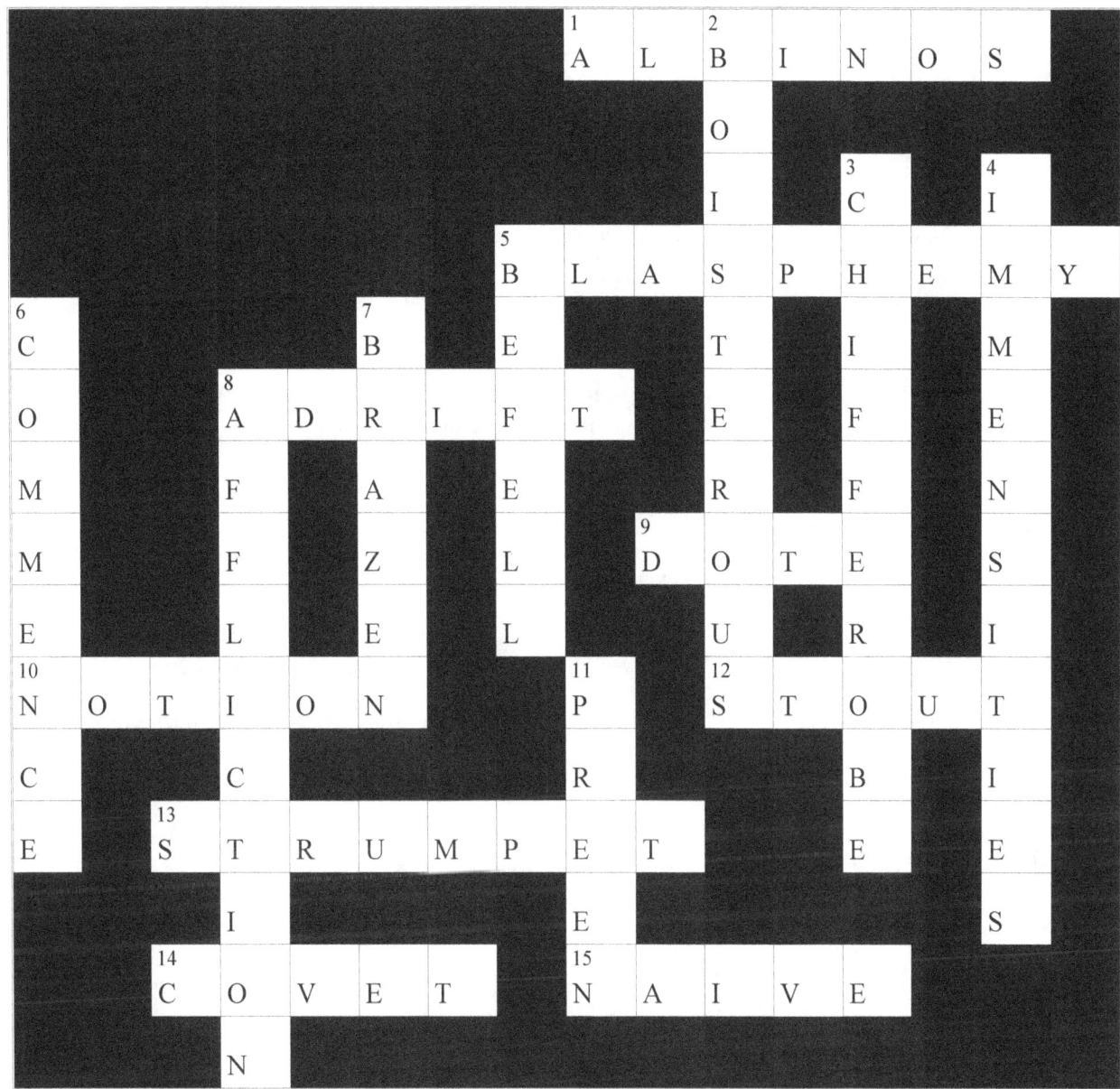

Across
1. People or animals with abnormally pale skin & hair
5. An act of cursing or speaking against God
8. Without direction or purpose
9. Show excessive fondness or love
10. Idea
12. Bulky in figure; heavily built
13. Prostitute
14. Wish for longingly
15. Lacking worldly experience and understanding; lacking sophistication

Down
2. Rough and noisy; noisily jolly or rowdy
3. Type of furniture having both drawers and space for hanging clothes
4. Vastness, boundlessness
5. Happened or occurred
6. Begin; start
7. Defiant; shameless
8. A condition of pain, suffering, or distress
11. Take pride or satisfaction in oneself; gloat

VOCABULARY MATCHING 1 *The Color Purple*

____ 1. VERBOSITY   A. Inclined to make trouble

____ 2. NAIVE   B. Of chief concern or importance

____ 3. IMMENSITIES   C. People who eat or consume immoderate amounts of food

____ 4. GLUTTONS   D. Without direction or purpose

____ 5. FRACTIOUS   E. Made holy

____ 6. DROVES   F. Search thoroughly by handling, turning over, or disarranging contents

____ 7. CONSCIENTIOUS   G. Similarity in appearance

____ 8. COMMENCE   H. Rough and noisy; noisily jolly or rowdy

____ 9. ADRIFT   I. Begin; start

____ 10. OSTRACISM   J. Large fishing net made to hang vertically in the water by weights at the lower edge and floats at the top

____ 11. PARAMOUNT   K. Gloomy, dark, depressing, extremely serious

____ 12. SULK   L. Meticulously careful; dutiful

____ 13. STOUT   M. Wordiness

____ 14. SOMBER   N. Bulky in figure; heavily built

____ 15. SEINING   O. Large crowds of human beings

____ 16. SANCTIFIED   P. Lacking worldly experience and understanding; lacking sophistication

____ 17. RUMMAGE   Q. Take pride or satisfaction in oneself; gloat

____ 18. RESEMBLANCE   R. Remain silent or hold oneself aloof in an ill-humored or offended mood

____ 19. PREEN   S. Vastness, boundlessness

____ 20. BOISTEROUS   T. The act of banishing or excluding

VOCABULARY MATCHING 1 ANSWER KEY *The Color Purple*

M	1.	VERBOSITY	A.	Inclined to make trouble
P	2.	NAIVE	B.	Of chief concern or importance
S	3.	IMMENSITIES	C.	People who eat or consume immoderate amounts of food
C	4.	GLUTTONS	D.	Without direction or purpose
A	5.	FRACTIOUS	E.	Made holy
O	6.	DROVES	F.	Search thoroughly by handling, turning over, or disarranging contents
L	7.	CONSCIENTIOUS	G.	Similarity in appearance
I	8.	COMMENCE	H.	Rough and noisy; noisily jolly or rowdy
D	9.	ADRIFT	I.	Begin; start
T	10.	OSTRACISM	J.	Large fishing net made to hang vertically in the water by weights at the lower edge and floats at the top
B	11.	PARAMOUNT	K.	Gloomy, dark, depressing, extremely serious
R	12.	SULK	L.	Meticulously careful; dutiful
N	13.	STOUT	M.	Wordiness
K	14.	SOMBER	N.	Bulky in figure; heavily built
J	15.	SEINING	O.	Large crowds of human beings
E	16.	SANCTIFIED	P.	Lacking worldly experience and understanding; lacking sophistication
F	17.	RUMMAGE	Q.	Take pride or satisfaction in oneself; gloat
G	18.	RESEMBLANCE	R.	Remain silent or hold oneself aloof in an ill-humored or offended mood
Q	19.	PREEN	S.	Vastness, boundlessness
H	20.	BOISTEROUS	T.	The act of banishing or excluding

VOCABULARY MATCHING 2 *The Color Purple*

____ 1. SABOTAGE   A. Radiating or reflecting light; shining; bright

____ 2. DIGNITY   B. Underhanded interference

____ 3. CONJURE   C. Hard-working

____ 4. CHIFFEROBE   D. Loud howling, wailing, or lamenting

____ 5. ADRIFT   E. Amends for wrong or injury done

____ 6. APTITUDE   F. Quality of being worthy of respect

____ 7. ULULATION   G. Oppressed; trampled upon

____ 8. TEDIOUS   H. Type of furniture having both drawers and space for hanging clothes

____ 9. SOJOURN   I. Capability; ability

____ 10. DOWNTRODDEN   J. Show or demonstrate plainly; reveal

____ 11. ENCROACHMENTS   K. Calm, peaceful, or tranquil

____ 12. REPARATIONS   L. Having or exhibiting religious reverence; devout

____ 13. PIOUS   M. Bring to mind; recall

____ 14. OVERABUNDANT   N. The treatment of guests and strangers in a warm, friendly, generous way

____ 15. MANIFEST   O. Without direction or purpose

____ 16. LUMINOUS   P. Tiresome by reason of length, slowness, or dullness

____ 17. INDUSTRIOUS   Q. More than is needed

____ 18. HOSPITALITY   R. A temporary stay

____ 19. FRETTING   S. Taking another's possessions or rights gradually or stealthily

____ 20. SERENE   T. Worrying

VOCABULARY MATCHING 2 ANSWER KEY *The Color Purple*

B	1.	SABOTAGE	A.	Radiating or reflecting light; shining; bright
F	2.	DIGNITY	B.	Underhanded interference
M	3.	CONJURE	C.	Hard-working
H	4.	CHIFFEROBE	D.	Loud howling, wailing, or lamenting
O	5.	ADRIFT	E.	Amends for wrong or injury done
I	6.	APTITUDE	F.	Quality of being worthy of respect
D	7.	ULULATION	G.	Oppressed; trampled upon
P	8.	TEDIOUS	H.	Type of furniture having both drawers and space for hanging clothes
R	9.	SOJOURN	I.	Capability; ability
G	10.	DOWNTRODDEN	J.	Show or demonstrate plainly; reveal
S	11.	ENCROACHMENTS	K.	Calm, peaceful, or tranquil
E	12.	REPARATIONS	L.	Having or exhibiting religious reverence; devout
L	13.	PIOUS	M.	Bring to mind; recall
Q	14.	OVERABUNDANT	N.	The treatment of guests and strangers in a warm, friendly, generous way
J	15.	MANIFEST	O.	Without direction or purpose
A	16.	LUMINOUS	P.	Tiresome by reason of length, slowness, or dullness
C	17.	INDUSTRIOUS	Q.	More than is needed
N	18.	HOSPITALITY	R.	A temporary stay
T	19.	FRETTING	S.	Taking another's possessions or rights gradually or stealthily
K	20.	SERENE	T.	Worrying

VOCABULARY JUGGLE LETTERS 1 *The Color Purple*

_____ = 1. ESYTORBVI
Wordiness

_____ = 2. TAFNCIOFIL
A condition of pain, suffering, or distress

_____ = 3. ERBFOCIFEH
Type of furniture having both drawers and space for hanging clothes

_____ = 4. NRUJECO
Bring to mind; recall

_____ = 5. HSNCCREANMOET
Taking another's possessions or rights gradually or stealthily

_____ = 6. IROFTHHRGT
Direct and straightforward

_____ = 7. TGONTSUL
People who eat or consume immoderate amounts of food

_____ = 8. TSSINMIMIEE
Vastness, boundlessness

_____ = 9. ATMNSFIE
Show or demonstrate plainly; reveal

_____ = 10. SSIRAOMCT
The act of banishing or excluding

_____ = 11. RCENAUGNPE
Strong distaste or objection

_____ = 12. UGAEMMR
Search thoroughly by handling, turning over, or disarranging contents

_____ = 13. SGEOTABA
Underhanded interference

_____ = 14. EIPSFLUT
Desiring to harm, annoy, frustrate, or humiliate another person

_____ = 15. SBEMALPHY
An act of cursing or speaking against God

VOCABULARY JUGGLE LETTERS 1 ANSWER KEY *The Color Purple*

VERBOSITY = 1. ESYTORBVI
Wordiness

AFFLICTION = 2. TAFNCIOFIL
A condition of pain, suffering, or distress

CHIFFEROBE = 3. ERBFOCIFEH
Type of furniture having both drawers and space for hanging clothes

CONJURE = 4. NRUJECO
Bring to mind; recall

ENCROACHMENTS = 5. HSNCCREANMOET
Taking another's possessions or rights gradually or stealthily

FORTHRIGHT = 6. IROFTHHRGT
Direct and straightforward

GLUTTONS = 7. TGONTSUL
People who eat or consume immoderate amounts of food

IMMENSITIES = 8. TSSINMIMIEE
Vastness, boundlessness

MANIFEST = 9. ATMNSFIE
Show or demonstrate plainly; reveal

OSTRACISM = 10. SSIRAOMCT
The act of banishing or excluding

REPUGNANCE = 11. RCENAUGNPE
Strong distaste or objection

RUMMAGE = 12. UGAEMMR
Search thoroughly by handling, turning over, or disarranging contents

SABOTAGE = 13. SGEOTABA
Underhanded interference

SPITEFUL = 14. EIPSFLUT
Desiring to harm, annoy, frustrate, or humiliate another person

BLASPHEMY = 15. SBEMALPHY
An act of cursing or speaking against God

VOCABULARY JUGGLE LETTERS 2 *The Color Purple*

_____ = 1. UVCHO
Guarantee; certify; attest to

_____ = 2. REOSSUTIOB
Rough and noisy; noisily jolly or rowdy

_____ = 3. COTEONCCD
Prepared by mixing ingredients

_____ = 4. UINNCCEOISOST
Meticulously careful; dutiful

_____ = 5. RLPEEYMXA
Worthy of imitation as a good example

_____ = 6. UCTFOSIAR
Inclined to make trouble

_____ = 7. FNIFCENEEDRI
Attitude of not caring one way or another

_____ = 8. OUULNSIM
Radiating or reflecting light; shining; bright

_____ = 9. EMITFNAS
Show or demonstrate plainly; reveal

_____ = 10. RPMNOTAUA
Of chief concern or importance

_____ = 11. TOISAENPRAR
Amends for wrong or injury done

_____ = 12. MECLSRNEAEB
Similarity in appearance

_____ = 13. RSOUNOJ
A temporary stay

_____ = 14. LATULNIUO
Loud howling, wailing, or lamenting

_____ = 15. FFONICTAIL
A condition of pain, suffering, or distress

VOCABULARY JUGGLE LETTERS 2 ANSWER KEY *The Color Purple*

VOUCH	= 1.	UVCHO Guarantee; certify; attest to
BOISTEROUS	= 2.	REOSSUTIOB Rough and noisy; noisily jolly or rowdy
CONCOCTED	= 3.	COTEONCCD Prepared by mixing ingredients
CONSCIENTIOUS	= 4.	UINNCCEOISOST Meticulously careful; dutiful
EXEMPLARY	= 5.	RLPEEYMXA Worthy of imitation as a good example
FRACTIOUS	= 6.	UCTFOSIAR Inclined to make trouble
INDIFFERENCE	= 7.	FNIFCENEEDRI Attitude of not caring one way or another
LUMINOUS	= 8.	OUULNSIM Radiating or reflecting light; shining; bright
MANIFEST	= 9.	EMITFNAS Show or demonstrate plainly; reveal
PARAMOUNT	= 10.	RPMNOTAUA Of chief concern or importance
REPARATIONS	= 11.	TOISAENPRAR Amends for wrong or injury done
RESEMBLANCE	= 12.	MECLSRNEAEB Similarity in appearance
SOJOURN	= 13.	RSOUNOJ A temporary stay
ULULATION	= 14.	LATULNIUO Loud howling, wailing, or lamenting
AFFLICTION	= 15.	FFONICTAIL A condition of pain, suffering, or distress

www.ingramcontent.com/pod-product-compliance
Lightning Source LLC
LaVergne TN
LVHW081532060526
838200LV00048B/2063